LIBRARY
LICENSING

LIBRARY LICENSING

A Manual for Busy Librarians

Corey Halaychik and
Blake Reagan

LIBRARIES
UNLIMITED®

An Imprint of ABC-CLIO, LLC

Santa Barbara, California • Denver, Colorado

Library of Congress Cataloging-in-Publication Data

Names: Halaychik, Corey S., author. | Reagan, Blake, author.
Title: Library licensing : a manual for busy librarians / Corey Halaychik and Blake Reagan.
Description: Santa Barbara, California : Libraries Unlimited, 2019. | Includes bibliographical references and index.
Identifiers: LCCN 2019030792 (print) | LCCN 2019030793 (ebook) | ISBN 9781440870767 (paperback) | ISBN 9781440870774 (ebook)
Subjects: LCSH: Letting of contracts—United States. | License agreements—United States. | Government purchasing—Law and legislation—United States. | Library administration—United States. | Librarians—United States—Handbooks, manuals, etc.
Classification: LCC KF850 .H35 2019 (print) | LCC KF850 (ebook) | DDC 344.73/092—dc23
LC record available at https://lccn.loc.gov/2019030792
LC ebook record available at https://lccn.loc.gov/2019030793

ISBN: 978-1-4408-7076-7 (paperback)
        978-1-4408-7077-4 (ebook)

24 23 22 21 20   1 2 3 4 5

This book is also available as an eBook.

Libraries Unlimited
An Imprint of ABC-CLIO, LLC

ABC-CLIO, LLC
147 Castilian Drive
Santa Barbara, California 93117
www.abc-clio.com

This book is printed on acid-free paper ∞

Manufactured in the United States of America

The authors would like to thank Kenneth A. Adams (author) and the Business Law Section (publisher) of the American Bar Association for granting us permission to use portions of their excellent book, *A Manual of Style for Contract Drafting, Fourth Edition*. Chicago, IL: American Bar Association, Business Law Section (2017), by Kenneth A. Adams.

Corey Halaychik would like to dedicate this book to the following individuals:

Rita, for being my favorite.

The DM, Belit, Linnear, and Annastrianna for all the hijinks, adventure, and banter that Kuzlo could ever wish for.

And Hastur, for freeing me from my earthly shackles.

Blake Reagan would like to dedicate the book to the following individuals:

Robert "Robbie" Pryor Jr., for motivating me to overcome my (former) fear of public speaking.

Ben Luttrell, for having the strongest meme game.

And my cats, for tolerating me.

Contents

Chapter 1   Introduction   1

Overview   1

What Is a Contract?   2

Why Are Contracts Important?   4

How Can Contracts Be Improved?   4

Technology   5

Language   5

Internal Review Process   6

Signature Authority   6

Mind-set   6

Chapter 2   Contract Language   9

Introduction   9

Contract-Management Software   10

Integrated Library Systems   13

Common Contract Clauses with Things to Consider   15

Introductory Clause   15

Recitals/Background   16

Term (Duration/Renewal) and Termination   16

Transactions   19

Financial Considerations 23

Pricing Models 29

Conclusion 40

Chapter 3 Organizing Contracts 43

Introduction 43

Terms Common in Library Licenses and Subscriptions 43

Access and Authentication 43

Accessibility 44

Archiving and Preservation 44

Consortia Purchases 45

Copyright 45

Course Packs/Electronic Reserves/Virtual Learning
Environments 45

Geographical/Institution/Unified Campus 46

Informing Authorized Users of Limitations 46

Interlibrary Loan 46

Monitoring and Reporting Misuse 47

Patron Record Maintenance 47

Return of/Destruction of Materials 47

Supplying Patron Records 48

Usage Statistics 48

Walk-In Users 49

General Clauses 49

Assignment 49

Attorneys' Fees 50

Automatic Renewal 52

Collection Costs 53

Court Costs 55

Counterparts 56

Dispute Resolution 56

Entire Agreement (Merger or Integration) 57

Exclusivity 58

Force Majeure (Acts of God) 60

Governing Law 62

Indemnification 63

Insurance 65

Limitation of Action 67

Liquidated Damages 68

Modification Waiver (or Amendment) 69

Multiple Languages 70

Nonsolicitation 70

Notice 72

Online Terms 73

Primary Vendor 77

Requirements 78

Severability 79

Supplier Conduct 79

Third-Party Beneficiary 81

Termination/Cancellation 81

Venue (or Jurisdiction or Forum Selection) 81

Conclusion 82

Chapter 4 Managing Contracts 85

Introduction 85

Specific Transactions and Special Topics 85

Intellectual Property 85

Confidentiality Agreements 87

Credit and Direct Bill Applications 88

Hotels 89

Maintenance Agreements 93

Catering 93

Image Release/Property Release   94

Performers, Speakers, Lecturers, and Others   94

Residential Leases for the Benefit of Students or Employees   96

Public Records   96

Conclusion   97

Chapter 5   Administering Contracts   99

Introduction   99

Contract Organization   99

Title   100

Introductory Clause   100

Recitals   101

Lead-in   101

Body   102

Signature Blocks   102

Attachments   102

Negotiating   103

Data Entry and Software   108

Exception Memos   109

Terminations   110

Conclusion   112

Chapter 6   Conclusion   115

Appendix A: Contract Review Checklist   117

Appendix B: Model Standard Payable Contract   129

Appendix C: Sample Visitor Hotel Rate Agreement   135

Appendix D: Sample Preferred Hotel Agreement   141

Appendix E: Sample Master Lease for Students   151

Appendix F: Sample Standard Amendment   161

Appendix G: Sample Professional Service Contract   163

Index   169

1

Introduction

OVERVIEW

Contracts are not scary or impossible. And contracts do not have to be difficult (contracts can be easy!). During our combined professional experience, the authors have encountered many people who are intimidated by, and even afraid of, contracts. The fear is understandable and reasonable. Unless you went to law school or you have spent significant amounts of time studying technical writing, contracts probably seem like a mysterious—even an impenetrable—world. The authors intend to help you lose your fear and approach contracts with confidence.

Perhaps you are not afraid of contracts—instead, you find contracts to be difficult or confusing. Perhaps you do not know where to start when it comes to improving your skills. In moments of frustration, you might have thought, "I need to go to law school." While no book could be a replacement for a graduate-degree program, you do not have to be an attorney to be good with contracts. The authors have observed a prominent pattern: most attorneys are very bad at contract drafting. Because of that reality, the authors encourage you to never feel intimidated by another party's legal counsel or even your own legal counsel.

We intend for this book to provide you with highly practical and actionable information. We hope that this book will allow you to do two things: first, strengthen your understanding of common contract clauses and issues; and, second, provide you with a starting point to create internal guidelines for your organization—a "contract manual," so to speak. We also hope to introduce you to resources that you can use to advance your contract-review and contract-drafting skills.

Whether or not you are intimidated by contracts, you almost certainly share the authors' frustration with the general lack of contract training available to nonattorneys. One of the co-authors is an attorney, and he has found there to be very few quality training classes available for attorneys. Although the authors do not claim to have conducted an exhaustive search, based on a reasonable amount of searching, the authors believe that training classes marketed toward nonattorneys are essentially nonexistent—or at least are very hard to find.

A full exploration into why most attorneys are not very skilled when it comes to contracts exceeds the scope of this book. For an authoritative book on contract language (which also addresses the root causes behind why most attorneys struggle with contract language), the authors highly recommend that you refer to *A Manual of Style for Contract Drafting, Fourth Edition,* by Kenneth A. Adams.[1] Further, we recommend Mr. Adams's seminars[2] (which are marketed toward attorneys, but, as of the date of this writing, are available to the general public). Further, Mr. Adams's website, www.adams drafting.com, is an excellent resource for enhancing your skills and knowledge about contract language. Mastering contract review requires mastery of contract drafting. In the authors' opinions, Mr. Adams's books, seminars, and website provide the best guidance for contract drafting.

You do not need any legal training to be good at reviewing contracts. There are very few "magic" (special) words or phrases in the law as it relates to contracts, so we encourage you to approach contracts in the same way you would approach any technical writing: with careful thought and analysis. If you have strong English-language skills and strong critical-thinking skills, you have the potential to be excellent at contract drafting, review, and other related tasks. Mastering contract review and drafting takes dedicated practice and thoughtful study.

WHAT IS A CONTRACT?

Stated in simple terms, a contract is a promise that the law will enforce.[3] Parties enter into contracts for many reasons, but at their core, contracts serve the following basic functions:

- Define the relationship between the parties (e.g., who will do what, when, where, and how)
- Allocate risk between the parties (i.e., who will bear the risk of certain actions or contingencies)
- Clearly outline the business transaction in an attempt to avoid misunderstanding or miscommunication, which will almost certainly result in harming the parties' relationship and might result in litigation

For the purposes of this book, we will assume that all contracts are written (whether electronic or hard copy). Although verbal agreements can constitute enforceable contracts, the details of when verbal agreements constitute enforceable contracts exceed the scope of this book. Furthermore, a business best practice is to have all agreements in writing, as it makes clear the expectations of the parties involved. Vendors may promise you things verbally, but you should ensure that you get all of the promises in writing in the contract that you sign.

Contract titles are important, but it is worth nothing that sometimes people overthink the title of documents, which is unnecessary. It does not matter whether your document is called an agreement, a memorandum of understanding, an order form, a purchase order, or something else. All of these documents are legally binding, and the authors consider all of these documents to be contracts. Please note that some end users at your organization might fall into the trap of thinking that the title of a document governs whether it is a contract. The authors have observed some departmental end users say something along the lines of, "This document is not a contract because its title is 'agreement.'"

We will further assume that your contracts are enforceable. Thus, we assume that your contracts meet the fundamental criteria to form a legally enforceable contract:

- *Offer:* One party (the offeror) makes it clear that they are willing to engage in a contract based on certain terms, if the other party accepts.

  An example of something that is not an offer is most advertisements, for example, the famous case of *Leonard v. Pepsico, Inc.*,[4] where the plaintiff claimed that Pepsi's commercial featuring a Harrier jet in exchange for 7,000,000 "Pepsi Points" was an offer. The court held that the commercial was mere puffery (i.e., a subjective statement made with the intention of serving as marketing, as opposed to an objective statement, which a reasonable person could take literally).

- *Acceptance:* The party receiving the offer accepts the offer completely.

  An example of an action that does not constitute acceptance is a counteroffer. Once a party makes a counteroffer, the previous offer is "dead," and the party making the counteroffer cannot metaphorically go back in time and accept the previous offer if the offeror rejects the counteroffer.

- *Consideration:* Although consideration is usually money, consideration could be many other things, provided that at least one party makes a promise to engage in conduct it is legally allowed to do or makes a promise to refrain from conduct that it is otherwise legally allowed to do.

  An example of something that is not valid consideration is if someone promised to refrain from using illegal drugs in exchange for something. Because the person is not legally allowed to use illegal drugs, their promise to refrain from illegal drugs is not consideration because the person does not have the *ability to use the drugs.*

- *Transaction is legal:* The transaction itself must be legal.

  An example of a promise that the law would not enforce is if an offeror attempted to contract to sell illegal drugs.

- *Parties are legally able to contract:* The parties must be adults and otherwise legally able to contract.

     An example of a promise that the law would not enforce is a minor promising to sell a car for a certain amount.

We will further assume that the reader is an employee of a library or affiliated office, such as procurement, contracts, legal, or something similar. This book will be useful for anyone who reviews contracts for any organization, especially people who have never received any training, whether through formal, postsecondary education or otherwise. The authors' work experience has been with academic libraries and government organizations. We will further assume that the reader will encounter many different types of contracts in their position, and thus, we will provide a wide range of information in this book.

Before we move on, it is worth noting that some people might assume that electronic terms listed on websites, order forms, and so on are not legally binding, or at least are not as enforceable as a normal contract where both parties sign. Although there have been some instances where courts refused to enforce terms listed on a website, you must assume that such terms are both binding and legally enforceable.[5] Therefore, the authors strongly recommend that you pay close attention to whether the vendors with whom you interact have terms on their websites. The odds are very high that most vendors with whom librarians work will have terms on their websites. The authors suggest you address those terms when entering into mutually signed contracts with a vendor or when your organization's authorized official signs order forms.

WHY ARE CONTRACTS IMPORTANT?

Contracts are important for many reasons. One significant reason is because contracts place your organization at risk for litigation. For that reason, it is especially important to review, revise, and draft contracts carefully.

Another important aspect of contracts is that they define the goods or services you will obtain from a vendor, at what amount, at what price, and sometimes at what quality. Contracts will govern what resources you can provide to your stakeholders and the limits on those resources. Moreover, contracts will help serve as the baseline for your organization's relationships with vendors directly and with stakeholders indirectly.

HOW CAN CONTRACTS BE IMPROVED?

It is best to think about contracts as you would any other business process or practice. Most organizations implement at least some improvements for their business processes, but most organizations fail to apply any process improvements to their contracts,[6] which is ironic, given the importance of both contracts and business processes.

Technology

The contracts that you will encounter will either be electronic or hard copy. Hard copies are a relic from the past, at least for organizations based in the United States. Other than "we have always done things this way" (which is never a valid reason to continue anything), there are no reasons for an organization to prefer hard copies. We recommend that your organization immediately switch from hard copies to electronic copies as a way to avoid imposing unnecessary costs on your organization, both in terms of time (soft costs) and supplies/services (hard costs) (e.g., postage, ink, envelopes, etc.).

If your organization does not have contract-management software, the authors recommend that you encourage appropriate officials at your organization to explore various options and purchase software that will allow your organization to process contracts more efficiently. And although no contract-management software is perfect, good options are available, and most options are far superior to paper-based contract processes.

Regarding contract signatures, the authors recommend that your organization adopt a software solution, such as DocuSign. There are other electronic-signature solutions, but the authors do not have experience with those. We encourage you to explore available options and obtain the solution that works best for your organization.

Microsoft Word and Adobe DC are common software programs that you will need to learn at an intermediate or advanced level if you work with contracts often. Many free tutorials on these products are available on YouTube and other websites.

Language

In the event you find yourself needing to draft contracts or edit clauses, the authors recommend that you refer to Adams's *A Manual of Style for Contract Drafting, Fourth Edition* (MSCD) as the authoritative source for contract drafting best practices. In the MSCD, Adams provides in-depth discussions on all topics that are relevant to improving your contract drafting, such as how to avoid ambiguity or vagueness. In our opinion, the MSCD is intended to be read by attorneys and contract professionals, but the book is insightful and provides valuable guidance to anyone involved in reviewing, revising, negotiating, or drafting contracts. So, the authors encourage you to review MSCD often to ensure that you are familiar with the best practices of contract drafting.

Internal Review Process

Improving internal review processes involves multiple considerations, such as the queue design, how many people are involved in the review process, how your organization communicates requested changes to a vendor, and relationships with internal stakeholders (such as audit, accounts payable, purchasing/procurement, etc.). For the purposes of this book, we will only focus on your organization's process as it relates to interacting with vendors. If you would like to expand your knowledge of improvement methodology, the authors recommend learning more about Lean Six Sigma.

Signature Authority

A common problem with large organizations (especially higher education entities) is signature authority. Usually, organizations will have official bylaws, a charter, policies, rules, and so on, which define who has authority to sign what documents. The larger an organization is and the less decentralized it is, the more difficult it will be to communicate correct signature authority rules.

The authors recommend creating a website in which you list all of the authorized officials by name and title and their corresponding signature authority. As with any official publication, it is best to list a version number and the date the page was last updated.

Mind-set

One way that your contract process can be improved is by changing your own mind-set. If you find contracts intimidating or impossible to understand, try to let go of that fear. Another mind-set change is to approach contracts like any other business process: with the idea of continuous learning and continuous improvement. Contracts do not need to be intimidating or overwhelming, and devoting time to better understand how they work, how they are written, and what they mean will help you become more confident and competent when working with them.

NOTES

1. Adams, Kenneth A., *A Manual of Style for Contract Drafting* (4th ed.), Chicago: American Bar Association, Business Law Section, 2017.
2. Adams, Kenneth A., "Public Seminars." Adams on Contract Drafting, www.adamsdrafting.com/speaking/public-seminars
3. Although this concept is stated in numerous sources, Blake would like to thank his first-semester contracts professor, George Kuney, for this definition. Professor Kuney's teaching style and content provided Blake with the initial

motivation to start him on the path to a career-long study of contract-drafting best practices.

4. 88 F. Supp. 2d 116 (S.D.N.Y. 1999), aff'd 210 F.3d 88 (2d Cir. 2000).
5. See the Electronic Frontier Foundation's website for more information. Electronic Frontier Foundation, "The Clicks That Bind: Ways Users 'Agree' to Online Terms of Service," https://www.eff.org/wp/clicks-bind-ways-users -agree-online-terms-service.
6. Adams, *A Manual of Style for Contract Drafting*, p. xxxvi.

2

Contract Language

INTRODUCTION

This chapter will provide information and recommendations for numerous types of contract clauses. The chapter is organized as follows: we address basic clauses that appear in almost all contracts, regardless of the nature of the contract. Next, we address common clauses that appear in various types of transaction-specific contracts. As applicable, we also discuss transaction-specific tips and things to consider.

The coauthors' intent is worth restating here: we intend for this book to be a starting point in your journey to improve your contract-review, contract-drafting, and contract-management skills. Throughout this book, we cite other resources. We highly recommend that you utilize the resources we cite because those resources go into much more detail in specific areas. While we briefly discuss confidentiality agreements, some authors have written entire books on confidentiality agreements. The same is true for hotel contracts.

For the purposes of our analysis in the sections that follow, we assume that your organization primarily reviews and processes a contract document that a vendor provides. Even if your organization only uses organization-drafted templates, this information will still be useful because vendors will often push back on templates other than their own documents.

Because many libraries are housed within government organizations, it is also useful to provide a short background on the concept of sovereign immunity. In simple terms, sovereign immunity is the concept that the government (the sovereign) gets to decide when, where, how, and for what it may be sued. In other words, because of sovereign immunity, the government may only be sued for claims it allows and only in the forums (courts or similar bodies) it allows.[1] Learning whether your organization has sovereign immunity is very important. If you work for a government organization, please consult with your legal counsel to determine the statutes that govern your organization's sovereign immunity. It is worth noting that sovereign immunity is a concept that not all attorneys are familiar with, perhaps because some law schools do not spend much time on the issue.

Before we get to the contract-language items, we will briefly discuss contract-management software.

CONTRACT-MANAGEMENT SOFTWARE

Numerous contract-management software options are available. An in-depth focus on contract-management software exceeds the scope of this book, but we will briefly discuss some points your organization might consider when evaluating contract-management software options.

A contract-management software solution platform serves to allow your organization to track its contracts as they move throughout the drafting and review stages. Additionally, the software can store its contracts and supporting documents for future reference. Choosing a contract-management software solution that fits your organization is important, and because every organization is unique, you should consider asking several questions as you explore the various software programs that exist. We recommend asking and considering the following:

- Will the software integrate with your other existing software systems, especially your organization's enterprise resource planning (ERP) software?
  - If so, how long will integration take?
  - How will integration occur?
  - How much manual effort will be required to maintain the data feeds and other system-to-system connections?
- Will your organization transfer previous contract-management records to the new contract-management software?
  - What records will you be able to transfer?
  - How long will you have access to the previous system?
  - Will all data (including workflow history, etc.) transfer over?
- Which system will be the "system of record" for contracts: the contract-management system, your organization's ERP system, or another system?
- Where is the data stored? Who has access to the data?
- Will your organization have access to the data if it changes to a different contract-management system?
- How much customizing will your organization need to do with the software? Consider customizing very carefully. Although it might be

tempting to customize the software to match your organization's current processes, there are four important things to consider first:

- Have you evaluated your organization's processes recently?

  - Many organizations do not implement Lean Six Sigma or another process-improvement technique. Before you implement a software is a good time to reflect on your organization's current processes and practices.

  - While certain things must be customizable, such as workflows, other things might not need to be. The less you customize, the less complicated your system will be.

- Who will produce the training materials?

  - What will be the format of the training materials?

    - Videos

    - Digital documents

  - In general, the less customizing you do, the better. If you use an off-the-shelf software product, the software's creator will most likely maintain training materials for you.

  - Maintaining the training materials yourself can be challenging, so you should consider the following:

    - If the software is updated, you will have to ensure that you update your training materials to reflect the updates.

    - Your organization's end users might end up looking at the software manufacturer's training materials, which will result in confusion.

- Who will train end users initially?

  - If your organization is large, implementing a new software (often called "rolling out" the software or "going live") can be a very large undertaking. Many end users' skill levels will vary, from some who struggle with using a computer, to others who are very savvy. Developing training materials that move fast enough to keep advanced users engaged while moving slowly enough to prevent the less savvy users from feeling left behind is a major challenge.

  - Consider whether it would be cost-effective to hire a consultant to develop training materials and provide the initial end-user training. Utilizing your organization's existing staff might be tempting, but doing so will necessarily require you to either add to a staff member's existing duties or reallocate the staff member's time.

- Who will provide ongoing end-user support?

  - Similar to the initial training issue, providing ongoing support can be challenging. If your organization will support the system internally, perhaps consider the following:

    - Will your organization have a dedicated help desk? If so, will you have one phone number, one group email address, etc.? Centralizing the communication points might be the best practice so your organization has an idea of how many end users need support, what their issues are, etc. Group email addresses can be both very useful and frustrating. If your organization uses a group email address, be sure to establish written guidelines for how your support team will use the inbox.

- o Will your organization utilize practitioners to provide support, as opposed to help-desk staff? If so, this offers advantages and disadvantages. Practitioners would be able to handle questions that the help-desk staff probably cannot handle, but providing software support could end up being a major burden on the practitioners' time.

- How much of your organization's staff time will be involved in implementing the software? Many organizations do not ask this question when evaluating software options. Considering internal costs, such as the need to increase staff, opportunity costs for requiring staff to focus on the new software instead of existing projects, etc., are important considerations.

- If your organization is switching from one contract-management software to another, consider what will change. Often, even simple things might be different, such as workflow step names, status names (for example, active, in-review, draft, etc.), or similar items. Consider the impact on end users if the system varies substantially from the previous contract-management system.

- If your organization will support the contract-management system, consider requiring the appropriate staff to create a detailed, step-by-step manual for how to support the system. You want to avoid disruptions if those support staff members leave within a short time frame.

- Will the software be able to account for nonsolicitation, noncompete, or similar clauses?

- Will the software track contingency payments, such as cancellation fees?

- Will the contract-management system send automatic email notifications to end users? If so, what actions or events will result in notifications?

- o When a reviewer rejects or approves? When a contract expires?

- o What will happen to notifications if a user leaves your organization?

- o What will happen to notifications if a user changes roles within your organization?

- o What will happen to notifications if a user changes departments within your organization but maintains the same role for the new department?

- If the contract-management system has email functionality, will your organization use it? The best practice would be to keep email communication in one platform, such as Outlook or Gmail, as opposed to having emails in multiple platforms.

- Will all internal workflow steps be contained in the system?

- o Carefully consider all possible places where the contract will go internally.

- o Will your legal office agree to be in the workflow?

- o What other offices might be involved in reviewing?

- Can the contract-management system alert your organization if a contract has been in review (that is, not acted on) within a certain time frame?
- What type of security will the system have?
- Will the system track related documents and applicable expirations of each document, such as certificates of insurance, licenses, etc.?
- Will you need to integrate any related software, such as Adobe Sign or DocuSign?
  - If so, consider whether the contract-management software will notify you if the signature integration fails on a particular transaction.
  - Does the contract-management system use "tokens" to keep track of the signature integration? Tokens are a way for a software system to track issues,[2] and in this context, tokens allow a software system to track emails. If so, where is the token? If the token is in the subject line of an email, what happens if the other party changes the subject line?
- Does the company selling you the licenses own the software?
  - If not, your organization is dealing with a reseller. Be sure to determine that the reseller is an authorized reseller.
  - What happens if the reseller goes out of business?
  - What happens if the reseller is sold to a competitor of the software manufacturer?
- Does the software have third-party plugins that the reseller or manufacturer requires? If so, what happens if those third-party plugins break? How much control over those third-party plugins does the reseller or manufacturer have?

INTEGRATED LIBRARY SYSTEMS

Librarians should also consider how their organization's existing integrated library system (ILS) might be used to assist with contract management. This is especially true of the newer generation of ILSs, which have ever more robust licensing modules either included with the base model or which can be included as an additional feature. Regardless of how an ILS is used for contract management, it is important to understand the difference between a licensing module and contract-management software.

An ILS is designed to manage all aspects of a library's public and technical services functions, including circulation, acquisitions, cataloging, and the searchable catalog. In most instances, these separate functions are contained within modules that allow library employees to have access to the modules on an as-needed basis. For example, everyone may need access to the searchable catalog, but only technical services staff may need access to the acquisitions module. Many ILSs include a separate licensing module designed to assist with tracking the terms associated with any agreements. Newer ILSs also typically have additional functions that allow library staff to quickly view important terms, for example, interlibrary privileges or access for walk-in users. These newer systems will often include ways to track and set reminders for when electronic resources or serials are due for renewal.

Contract-management software, while sharing some of the same features as an ILS licensing module, is designed to facilitate the entire lifecycle of the contract review and approval process. Although this does result in some overlap of function, such as document storage, it means that contract-management software is more robust in functionality, including, at a minimum, the ability to track and share document versions throughout the editing process, facilitate the signing of documents, workflow automation, template creation, and the running of reports and analytics. Furthermore, many contract-management software suites have the ability to work with an application programming interface (API) to interface with other systems. This feature and the focus of API use by libraries for their ILS allow for the potential integration between both types of products. This would avoid the need for nonlibrary personnel to have access to library-specific systems while allowing library employees to use a system shared across an institution.

We recommend asking the following questions when evaluating use of an ILS licensing module in conjunction with contract-management software:

- Will the module integrate with other software systems being used by your organization to process contracts?
  - If so, how will the integration be handled?
  - How much manual effort will be required to maintain the data feeds and other system-to-system connections?
  - Who will be responsible for maintaining the data feeds?
  - Who within the library will have access to the contract-management software?
- Will previous contracts be transferred to the contract-management software? What records and information will you be able to transfer?
- Which system will be the "system of record" for contracts: the contract-management system or the licensing module?
- Will the library have access to records if it migrates to a new ILS?
- Have you evaluated your library's license review processes recently? Although a level of redundancy in workflows or record keeping might be tempting, revising workflows and reducing the number of systems being maintained can greatly improve efficiency.
- How often does your library and/or larger organization switch systems? Libraries are constantly evolving, but larger organizations that oversee libraries—like a large academic institution or municipal government—might not move as quickly. It is important to think about how upgrades to one system might affect interoperability among other departmental systems.
- If the licensing module includes renewal reminders, will your library use it or will it rely on the email functionality in the contract-management system? If

the renewal reminders are sent via email, to whom are the emails sent? What happens if someone changes jobs within the organization or leaves the organization? Determine whether the notification recipients must be maintained manually or whether the contract-management system will be able to update itself when human resource changes occur.

- Does the software have third-party plugins or APIs that are required for interoperability? If so, what happens if those third-party plugins or APIs have technical issues, and who will be responsible for working with the vendor to address the issues?

COMMON CONTRACT CLAUSES WITH THINGS TO CONSIDER

Introductory Clause

The introductory clause, as the name might suggest, is the first clause of every contract. Introductory clauses typically contain these elements:

- The title of the contract
- Legal names of the parties (including their legal structure)
- Defined term for each party (for example, "University," "Customer," "Seller," or "Contractor")
- Date of the agreement

Some commentators label the introductory clause the "preamble,"[3] but the purpose remains the same: to establish who the agreement is between and when the contract is established.

Example:
This digital content license agreement is dated January 1, 2020, and is between The University of Cats, an instrumentality of the state of Nevada, and Laser Pointer Enterprises, Inc., a California corporation.

Model introductory clause:[4]
This _____ [title of agreement] agreement is dated _____, 20__ and is between _____ [name of this entity], a/an [state of incorporation] [legal structure] ("name of this entity for purposes of this agreement"), and [name of this entity], a/an [state of incorporation] [legal structure] ("name of this entity for purposes of this agreement").

Notes:
- The introductory clause does not define the agreement (i.e. "this agreement"). There is no need to make the agreement itself a defined term because "this agreement" clearly refers to the agreement that the parties are entering into.[5]

- For similar reasons, we did not use "the Parties" or "the Party" as defined terms. The identities of the parties is a clear, and self-evident, concept. So, there is no reason to capitalize "parties" or "party" in a contract.

Recitals/Background

Generally speaking, a recitals section is not necessary for most contracts. Recitals, although not very common in many types of contracts, are still a common feature of certain types of contracts and therefore worth being familiar with. Generally, recitals are found in contracts that are long or complex,[6] The word "recitals" is not a magic word and is just contract language for background information. As such, the purpose of this section is to provide the reader with additional information to help the contract make sense in context. Recitals might be useful if your organization acquired the transaction through a public bid process, or if the contract relates to a cooperative/consortium arrangement or a similar situation where the context might not be readily apparent to the reader. Recitals might also be useful when a contract relates to one or more contracts.

Ken Adams notes that there are three general types of recitals: context recitals, purpose recitals, and simultaneous-transaction recitals.[7] For more information, see the *Manual of Style for Contract Drafting* (MSCD, 4th edition).[8] The authors do not intend for this book to provide contract-drafting guidance, so we will assume that you refer to the MSCD for contract-language guidance.

It is common for a contract to state that the recital section is incorporated by reference into the body of the contract.[9] This is a legacy practice, and because the best practice is to never include substantive provisions in a recitals section, you do not need to incorporate the recitals by reference.[10]

> *Example:*[11]
> **Background**
> - On September 15, 2018, the University of Cats issued a request for proposals #123456 ("RFP") through a public, competitive solicitation process.
> - The University of Cats issued an award through the RFP to Laser Pointer Enterprises on November 1, 2018.
> - Laser Pointer Enterprises and The University of Cats entered into a nondisclosure agreement on December 15, 2018.

Term (Duration/Renewal) and Termination

From the perspective of working in a large organization's procurement office, a good practice is to include the term of the agreement (start date and end date), renewals, and termination as the first clause of the contract—or at least include the clause very early in the contract. Large organizations typically have thousands of contracts, and being able to locate the term/duration clause quickly will help improve efficiency.

Start Date and End Date. Be sure to specify a start date and an end date. When you think about optimizing the agreement's duration, ensure that you have reviewed your organization's policies and procedures and applicable state law and have discussed this with all internal stakeholders. Of course, be sure to discuss the agreement's duration with the other party too. While not necessarily common, some vendors might not agree to a long-term contract. Stakeholder feedback might be particularly useful if the stakeholders have had negative experiences with the vendor. Stakeholders could also inform you about whether the good or service is critical, how easy it would be to replace the vendor, how quickly you could find competitors, and whether replacing the vendor would create substantial additional costs. Further, stakeholder feedback could provide you with guidance for when to structure the end date. For example, if the stakeholders need the service through February of each year, you would want to ensure that the contract expires on February 28 or later.

Standardizing the end date of all contracts to the last calendar day of a month will make it easier to manage renewals and expirations. Consider also whether it would be optimal to set the end date as the last calendar day of the month in which your fiscal year ends, the last calendar day of the calendar year, or the last calendar day of another month. It is also worth considering spacing out renewals when possible as a means to spread out workload throughout the year. In libraries, it is common for many serials subscriptions to run on a calendar basis with January 1 start and December 31 end dates. Although it might be appealing to set up all subscriptions with a common run date, it can create a needlessly heavy workload and burden on staff who are faced with processing renewals for serials, databases, and other subscriptions in a short window of time.

Other factors to consider when evaluating the duration of a contract include the following:

- Does state law address a contract's duration? If so, does state law allow for exceptions such that certain types of contracts might have longer durations? For government entities, if state law is silent, has the legislative area of your state's government expressed a preference regarding contract duration?
- Did the contract come from a procurement sourcing event, such as a request for proposals, invitation to bid, etc.? If so, generally speaking, the contract cannot exceed the length stated in the sourcing event.
- Will the good or service be integrated into another good or service? If so, the terms might need to be concurrent.
- Is the good or service related to another good or service?

Renewals. Before renewing a contract, be sure to check with stakeholders to ensure that the stakeholder wants to renew. It is a best practice to establish a mechanism to discuss renewals with stakeholders. This can take the form of an advisory committee that reviews subscriptions periodically, individual meetings with subject librarians, or annual surveys. How feedback is received is less important than ensuring that stakeholders are consulted on a regular basis and provide meaningful input.

The following are questions to consider when evaluating a contract's potential duration:

- What is the start date?
  - Is the start date workable for the end user?
  - Would a different start date be optimal?
- What is the end date?
  - Is the end date workable for the end user?
  - Would a different end date be optimal?
  - Is the end date the last day of a calendar month?
- Is your organization allowed to enter into the proposed term? For example, some state-government agencies are not allowed to enter into a contract that exceeds one year.
- Does the agreement renew automatically?
  - If so, is this allowable for your organization? Many state-government agencies cannot agree to automatic renewal.
  - How far in advance do you need to provide notice if you do not want to renew?
    - Does your organization have an ability to track notice periods?
    - How long will your organization be locked in if you fail to cancel within the allotted time?
- If the agreement does not automatically renew, what is the process for renewal?
- If you terminate the agreement early:
  - Will your organization receive a refund?
  - Will your organization have any obligations that extend after the early termination date?
  - Under what circumstances could your organization terminate?

Time. If you refer to time in a contract, be sure to think carefully about time zones. As of the date of this writing, the United States still uses Daylight Savings Time (DST) and Standard Time (ST). Those two different time schemes refer to specific periods (months during which one time or the other applies).

Many people loosely use the time periods when referring to a time zone.[12] For example, many people write "Eastern Standard Time" to refer to Eastern

Time 365 days a year, without recognizing that "Eastern Standard Time" actually refers to a specific period. The best practice is to refer to the time zone (for example, Pacific Time), without referring to the specific time period—for example, "Eastern Time," as opposed to writing, "Eastern Standard Time."

Also, consider that some jurisdictions do not observe one period or the other. Arizona, for example, does not observe DST (except the Navajo Nation within Arizona observes DST).[13] In this case, consider referring to the time in a particular city.[14] For example, consider referring to "5:00 PM, Phoenix time."

Transactions

Because the nature of transactions varies so much, it is not possible for the authors to anticipate the nature of the specific transactions you will encounter. Perhaps you are contracting with a hotel or caterer, or possibly a service company to maintain your printers and copy machines. Each transaction is different, but you can use good contract review and drafting principles to ensure that your contracts are clear and comprehensive, regardless of the subject matter.

Be sure to read (or draft) the contract carefully to ensure that the transaction is completely and accurately described in the document. You will need to ensure that the end users have read and understood the contract. If the contract requires end users to provide certain things or take certain actions, you must ensure that the end users can actually provide the things or take the actions.

Generally speaking, end users probably do not read contracts very closely. In the authors' experience, end users sometimes do not read contracts at all. While end users at your institution might be accustomed to actually reviewing draft contracts closely, the authors suggest that you never assume that the end users have read the contract. This recommendation stands even if you require end users to approve a contract as part of the organization's review process, and even if your organization requires end users to attest that they have read the contract. Many end users might feel unnecessarily intimidated by contracts, so they might not feel comfortable reading the contract at all. Some end users might have convinced themselves that they will never understand contracts. Also, some end users might mistakenly believe that the organization's contract-review staff members will understand the end users' needs and limitations. Generally speaking, contract-review staff almost never understand the end users' precise needs and limitations.

Ensuring end users have read and understood the contract is particularly important when it comes to the following types of contracts.[15] Consider creating a list of issues that arise in particular types of contracts. A sample is shown here.

Type of contract	Discussion items when interacting with end users
Library licenses	Ensure that the library can comply with access restrictions, notification requirements, data requirements, and interlibrary loan limitations.
Equipment	Ensure that the equipment is compatible with existing equipment or if the new item(s) will be connected to existing items. Ensure that the equipment will fit in the space provided. Will installing the equipment require changes to the building?
Exclusive agreements	Ensure that the exclusive agreement does not conflict with other exclusive agreements.
Hotel	Ensure that contract-review staff inform the end users of the consequences of attrition and cancellation clauses. Also, ensure that the end users limit the number of rooms reserved to a reasonable number. Often, end users book far too many rooms without considering the consequences.

Regardless of the contract's subject matter, you will want to ensure that all of your organization's contracts are accurate and complete (all of the vendor's promises are stated in the contract).

Service Contracts. Service contracts vary greatly and can range from utilities to consulting. Ensure that the contract addresses how the vendor will provide the service, when the vendor will provide the service, which staff members from the vendor will provide the service, if the vendor will subcontract any of the work, and where the vendor will provide the service. Further, consider what insurance the vendor will need to provide.

Many types of services require special licenses and permits. Ensure that the contract addresses the necessary permits and licenses specifically. Further, determine whether a performance bond, payment bond, or other type of bond is necessary. If so, be sure to include that in the contract as well. Consider, also, whether the vendor must provide proof of it obtaining the special licenses and permits when necessary. And, if so, when does the provider need to provide such proof? The best practice would be to ensure that the vendor provides such proof before your organization signs the contract or, at the latest, before the vendor starts work. If you allow the vendor to provide proof after your organization signs the contract, be sure to specify in the contract when the vendor must provide the licenses or permits. Also, be sure to specify what will happen if the vendor does not provide the licenses or permits.

Goods. Contracts for goods involve many of the same issues as service contracts, with the additional issues of shipping, returning goods, etc. Be sure to carefully review the contract to ensure you are familiar with these additional sections. For libraries, having a clear understanding of shipping and return requirements can help determine the best way to order materials while still being fiscally responsible. For example, does the cost of ordering an item "rush" make sense if the delivery date is not significantly reduced? Similarly, is there a mechanism for returning duplicate materials for a refund if a mistake is needed and far more copies of a book were ordered than actually needed?

Shipping Terms. An in-depth discussion of shipping terms exceeds the scope of this book, but we will provide some basic information next. Unfortunately, shipping terms are often overlooked because people assume that "FOB" (free on board) shipping means what they think it means. Also, many people assume that everything will be okay when it comes to shipping, and, worse, they often assume that the vendor will easily replace or repair items that are damaged during transit. When buying physical goods, it is important to consider shipping terms.

When you think about shipping, there are three scenarios you need to consider:

1. Drop-shipping: When a vendor uses third parties to fulfill an order and the third party ships the item to the customer on behalf of the vendor. For example, you might order from Acme Cartoon Widget Corporation, which uses a third-party company, Lucy's Chocolate Assembly Line, Inc., to fulfill the order. Even though you ordered the item from Acme, Lucy's will fulfill the order and ship directly to you. Drop-shipping essentially involves two different legal relationships: your contract with the vendor and the vendor's contract with the drop-shipper.[16] Almost always, the drop-shipper will use a third-party carrier. In this scenario, you have the following taking place:

   • Vendor selling the item to your organization.
   • Vendor placing the order with a third party.
   • Third party fulfilling the order and placing the item with a delivery company (such as a third-party carrier).
   • Third-party carrier delivers the item.

2. Vendor delivers: When the vendor uses vendor-owned transportation and vendor staff to deliver.

3. Third-party carrier delivers: When the vendor (or drop-shipper) uses a third-party carrier, such as FedEx or UPS.

For an in-depth look at shipping terms, the authors recommend Frank Reynolds's excellent work on the topic, *Incoterms for Americans*. Unfortunately, shipping terms are poorly understood in the United States. Globally, many countries other than the United States use the Incoterms.[17] In the United States, most organizations use the very misunderstood shipping term FOB.

To avoid the possibility of confusion, the authors recommend that you avoid using jargon of any kind when it comes to shipping. Instead, use standard English to describe the important elements of shipping.

When you draft shipping terms, consider the following:

- Who will arrange the shipping?
- Who will pay for shipping? Will the vendor list shipping as a line item on the invoice?
- When does risk of loss shift to your organization? The best-case scenario is for risk of loss to transfer to your organization when the goods are delivered to your organization.
- Does your organization want shipping insurance? If so, who will obtain it: your organization or the vendor? If the vendor obtains it, who is the beneficiary of the insurance? How do you file a claim?
- Will a third party deliver the items? Most of the time, a third-party carrier, such as FedEx, UPS, USPS, or DHL will deliver the items.
  - The third-party carriers generally require your organization to sign for delivery, and when someone from your organization signs for delivery, your organization usually waives the carrier's liability for damages. Be sure to state in your contract that the vendor remains responsible for the delivery and that your organization has a stated time frame after delivery during which it can report damages.
  - Declared value: If the vendor will use a third-party carrier, will the vendor declare the value of the shipment with the carrier?
- When does title transfer to your organization?
- How long will your organization have to inspect the shipment and report any damages to the vendor? Most of the time, vendors do not want your organization to have any time to report damages, so a vendor's standard contract will not allow for this period. You will need to negotiate with the vendor to ensure that you protect your organization. This is especially important for libraries who may see a delay in materials (books, computers, furniture, etc.) arriving at the final department because of a centralized shipping network, such as a central warehouse, where all shipments arrive before being shipped elsewhere.

Model language:

Shipping
    a. *Arrangement:* [which party] will arrange shipping goods to the customer's specified locations.
    b. *Costs:* [state who will pay for shipping].
    c. *Insurance:* [Will either party pay for insurance on the shipment? If so, will the coverage be for purchase price or replacement costs? Who is the beneficiary of the coverage?]
    d. *Third-party:* [applicable if a vendor will drop-ship items].
        i. *Reporting damages:* [State to whom customer will report damages. Generally, it's best if the customer reports damages to the vendor and the vendor would be responsible for working out any issues with the third-party shipper].

      ii. _Declared value_: [Requires the vendor to declare the value of the shipment with the third-party carrier, such as FedEx].

    e. _Title_: Customer takes title to the goods upon customer's physical receipt of goods.

    f. _Damages_: Vendor is responsible for all damages that occur during shipment, regardless of cause, until the customer takes title to the goods.

    g. _Inspection and rejection_: Customer may inspect the goods at any time from the point that the customer takes title to 14 calendar days later. Within the 14-day period, the customer may reject any goods without penalty by providing the vendor notice.

Financial Considerations

The financial aspect of your transactions is probably the area to which you and your business officers pay the most attention. Note that if you rely heavily on legal counsel to review contracts, many attorneys do not have a business mind-set and might not consider the business realities and risks involved.[18]

Beginning with the end in mind is a great practice for many things in life, and that is certainly true for contracts. Before you start negotiating the contract, be sure to think through all of the stakeholders' needs, including how your organization will ensure that the vendor has complied with the contract.

An important consideration is time. When it comes to rebates, pricing, etc., is the financial portion of your contract tied to a calendar year, contract year, or another year (such as the vendor's fiscal year)?

Here are some initial things to consider:

- Currency: What currency will your organization use to pay? As of the date of this writing, the U.S. dollar is the most commonly used currency in the world for international transactions. If your organization uses a currency other than your home country's currency, you are at risk for currency fluctuations. In other words, if your organization is in the United States and you agree to pay in Canadian dollars, your organization is taking a risk that the U.S. dollar will slip in value in comparison to the Canadian dollar; thus, the transaction could end up being more expensive than you agreed in the contract. Also, your organization will have to pay fees to have your U.S. dollars converted to Canadian dollars.

- Advanced payment: Will your organization need to make advanced payment to the vendor? If so, the best practice would be to conduct due diligence and research the background of the company.
  - Go to the company's website.
    - Is the website up-to-date?
    - Do all of the links work?
    - Is the contact information correct?

- How long has the company been in business?
- How many employees does the company have?
  - Be very cautious about making large advanced payments to small companies, especially start-ups.

The risk with advanced payment is that the vendor will take your organization's money but not deliver the goods or services. The cost to recover your organization's funds might be prohibitive, so carefully consider when your organization will allow advanced payment.

Costs. What types of costs will the vendor charge? The best practice is to ask the vendor to disclose all possible costs to your organization before you sign a contract with the vendor and to include a clause stating that the vendor must not charge your organization any costs unless the costs are specifically allowed under the contract. The following is a list of many types of costs that a vendor might charge:

- Cleaning fees
  - Do these vary?
  - How does the vendor determine the amount?
- Commissions
  - What is the rate?
- Customs/international fees
- Dealer fees
- Documentation fees
- Hazardous material fees
- Hourly fees or rates
  - Do these vary based on the nature of the representative from the vendor working on the project?
  - Do the rates vary if work is performed during certain hours or on certain days (such as weekends or holidays)?
- Gratuity
- Labor/installation
- Processing fees
- Profit (applicable in cost-plus pricing models)
- Restocking
- Return
- Rush order/expedited shipping
- Service fees
- Set-up fees (might be called "white glove service")
- Shipping/freight/logistics/delivery/transportation
- Surcharge

- Taxes applied
- Transaction fees
- Travel
  - Include in the amount what the vendor charges your organization (i.e., not a line item on an invoice).
  - Is it a flat rate (e.g., $300 per day—travel would appear as line item, but the flat rate covers all travel costs)?
  - Are the vendor's costs reimbursed?
    - Be sure to define the types of travel costs that your organization will not pay, such as rental car class above standard, airfare above economy, or parking other than the least expensive option (such as economy parking at an airport).
    - Requiring the vendor to provide receipts would be important so that you can verify the costs.

Standardizing business processes and documents is a basic best practice under Lean or Lean Six Sigma.[19] A good way to standardize your organization's ability to collect a vendor's cost information accurately would be to use a cost disclosure form, which the vendors would complete and return to you before you finalize the contract draft. An example form is shown next.

Cost Disclosure Form	
Please indicate whether your company will charge the customer any of the following costs.	
Please note that, if you fail to disclose a cost, the customer will not pay the cost.	

	Yes	No	State exactly how this fee will be calculated	State exactly how this fee will appear on invoices as a line item
Cleaning fees				
Commissions				
Customs/international fees				
Dealer fees				
Deposits				
Documentation fees				
Hazardous material fees				

(continued)

	Yes	No	State exactly how this fee will be calculated	State exactly how this fee will appear on invoices as a line item
Hourly fees				
Labor/installation				
Processing fees				
Profit				
Restocking				
Rush order/expedited shipping				
Service fees				
Shipping/freight/logistics				
Surcharge				
Taxes applied				
Transaction fees				
Travel				

For any fee not disclosed here, you must describe the fee:

Name of fee	How you will calculate the fee	How the fee will appear as a line item

Prohibited Costs. It might be worthwhile to specify that the vendor cannot charge any costs unless they are stated in the contract.

Model clause:
Prohibited costs: Vendor shall not charge customer any costs, unless the cost is explicitly stated in this agreement.

Pro Forma Invoice. Almost all vendors, if not all vendors, have an example of their invoice format with descriptions for charges that the vendor will provide to the customer. A best practice is to request a pro forma invoice for every vendor during the contract-negotiation process, and use the format and wording on the invoice to drive how you structure the contract.

For example, if the pro forma invoice lists digital content titles in a particular format, it would be best to mirror that format in the contract. This practice will reduce the risk of audit findings and will improve the ability of your organization's accounts payable function to pay the invoice without the need to seek additional documentation. Note that if a vendor uses a drop-shipper, it might be very difficult to get the vendor's invoice to match the drop-shipper's shipping documents. In other words, your vendor's invoice might state that you ordered Lucy's Best Chocolate Chips 2.0 (quantity of 1 box), but the drop-shipper's shipping documentation might show that you received Choc. Chip. #37950 (quantity of 1 at 12 oz.).

Using a pro forma invoice to drive how the contract will be worded will reduce confusion on the contract administration side. The invoices will match the contract, which will reduce potential problems when it comes to auditing, accounts payable, etc.

Payment Method. Be sure to specify how your organization will pay the vendor. Will your organization pay by automated clearing house (ACH) transfer, check, credit card, draft (for foreign entities), or wire? Please note that checks and wires are the most expensive ways to pay.

Time for Payment. When will your organization pay the vendor? The usual time for payment is within a set number of days after the vendor invoices the customer. If the vendor sends paper invoices via mail, consider how long it will take for the vendor to generate the invoice, print the invoice, place the invoice in an envelope, prepare the envelope for mailing, and place the envelope in the mail and for the post office to deliver the mail. If your organization is large and has its own mail services department, consider that time, too. The vendor might print the invoice on Monday, mail it on Tuesday, and it might arrive by Friday. Your organization has already lost five days of time to pay the invoice. Foreign vendors sending paper invoices from their home countries will also add considerable time to the invoices' arrival.

Be sure to specify when your organization will be required to pay the vendor. If payment is due within a date of the invoice, be sure to specify whether the date is the date that your organization receives the invoice or the date that the vendor issues the invoice.

- Your organization is better off if the date is the date that your organization receives the invoice. The reason is because you have no control over when the vendor will send the invoice.
- If the vendor insists that the date be the date on the invoice, be sure to ask the vendor to explain their invoicing process.
  - Will the vendor issue a paper invoice?
    - If so, how often does the vendor print and mail invoices?

- ▪ How long does it take for the printed invoice to reach the post office nearest the vendor (there could be several internal steps before the invoice leaves the vendor's building)?
  - ○ Will the vendor issue an electronic invoice?
    - ▪ If so, will the vendor also send a paper invoice? This would present a risk because the vendor sending the same invoice twice in two different ways (electronic and hard copy) would drastically raise the risk of overpayment.
    - ▪ Will your organization set up a generic email address to receive invoices? This would be better than the invoices going to specific individuals because the email address will stay the same, regardless of who is employed at your organization.

Pricing. The best practice is to review the vendor's pricing to ensure that it is easily calculable and verifiable. Be sure to check with your accounts payable department, auditors, and attorneys to ensure that you understand their needs when it comes to invoicing and payment.

Price Increases. Most contracts that extend beyond one year will contain a clause allowing the vendor to increase its pricing at a stated interval by an amount. Such clauses are often called "escalator" clauses. When you review an escalator clause, be sure to review it for 1) amount (can you afford the increase?) and 2) precision (is the amount precise or tied to a precise index?). The amount might be stated as a cap (e.g., "up to 5%"), a firm amount (e.g., "by 3.5%"), or tied to an index (e.g., "by the amount of CPI for All Urban Consumers published in January of each year").

In the United States, there is a federal government agency that issues Consumer Price Index (CPI) data to measure inflation. Many vendors tie annual price increases to CPI. The problem with referring to just CPI is that the U.S. Bureau of Labor Statistics (BLS) has multiple ways that it calculates the CPI. So, a vague reference to "CPI" allows the vendor to pick the one that reflects the highest amount. In actuality, the difference from one CPI to another usually only means a few dollars, but it's important to control costs and eliminate ambiguity from a contract. You can find more information on the BLS's website: http://www.bls.gov/cpi.

The BLS has the following types of CPI:

- All Urban Consumers
- Urban Wage Earners and Clerical Workers
- All Urban Consumers (Chained CPI)
- Average Price Data

An example of an unacceptable clause would be: "Any renewals will be subject to a 3% CPI increase." That language:

- Makes no sense because CPI is never forecasted in advance, and CPI does not mean "corporate cost of living" (the unacceptable language seeks to forecast CPI at 3%).

- Is vague. First, there are multiple types of CPI. Further, what does 3% CPI increase mean? Does it mean "3% increase over whatever CPI the vendor chooses?" A vendor could reasonably argue that the language means 3% plus CPI.

Pricing Models

In the authors' experience, many organizations overlook pricing models, but an organization that does so sets itself up for audit findings, overpayment, and other negative consequences. In this subsection, we will discuss various items related to pricing. Also, please note that for the purposes of this section, audit considerations ignore whether the price is a fair or reasonable market price. Determining whether a vendor has complied with contract pricing and determining whether the pricing is reasonable under the market are two very different concepts.

Determining whether a vendor has complied with contract pricing often means that your organization will need to check two different points in time: 1) the pricing that the vendor is charging in real time (e.g., your organization's office supplies contract) and 2) the pricing that the vendor already charged your company on a previous order.

Your organization's procurement, audit, accounts payable, or other similar office will need access to the vendor's catalog, online ordering portal, etc., to see the real-time pricing that the vendor is offering to your organization. You can improve transparency by allowing end users to see the contract pricing, because end users who are ordering items will already have access to the real-time pricing.

End users and others will need access to the contract pricing to be able to verify whether the pricing on a vendor's invoice matches the contract pricing. Verifying that a vendor's invoice matches the contract pricing is not as easy as it sounds.

Determining whether a vendor's pricing is reasonable under the market is a topic that exceeds the scope of this book. Many resources are available online (most are subscription-based software databases), and the authors have found that using public records laws is an effective way to determine what a vendor is charging government agencies. If your organization is a government agency, consider making public records requests to benchmark a vendor's pricing against what you are paying.

If your organization allows its employees to use procurement cards (organization credit cards), be sure to think about whether the vendor will be able to provide your organization with the correct contract pricing for those purchases. In the authors' experience, many organizations do not get to take full advantage of their contract pricing because most vendors do not have a way to ensure that the vendor provides the procurement cards with correct contract pricing. If your organization allows individuals to use procurement cards and your vendors do not store those procurement card numbers, the only way your employees will be able to access your negotiated pricing is to uniquely identify themselves as part of your organization. A common way to do that is to require employees to buy through your organization's ordering platform. Another way to do this is to ensure that employees provide the vendor with credentials that automatically apply the organization's negotiated pricing to the employee's purchase.

Your organization spends a lot of time and resources negotiating deals, but the authors are confident that most organizations fail to take advantage of their negotiated rates for a certain percentage of transactions: those transactions that the vendor does not, or cannot, identify as being affiliated with your organization.

In general, a vendor's pricing will follow one or more of these types of pricing models:

a) Firm/Fixed Pricing
b) Discounts
c) Cost Plus
d) Time and Materials

Before we move to the specifics of each pricing model, please keep in mind that with any contract, it is important to answer some basic questions:

1. How will your organization ensure that it gets the benefit of its negotiated contract?
2. How will the vendor be able to ensure that it complies with the contract?
3. How will the vendor identify spending from your organization?
4. Is it possible that your employees will be able to buy from the vendor without linking themselves to your organization's pricing?
5. What information will you have access to that will allow you to audit the vendor to ensure compliance?

A final note before we move on to the specifics of each pricing model: as of the date of this book's publication, the authors foresee a trend in pricing for goods that might drastically alter the market for goods in the foreseeable future. Rather than static pricing or even pricing models, due to the power, size, and scope of large retailers such as Amazon, it is possible that many organizations will shift their purchasing behavior for goods to buying at market pricing, as opposed to having set pricing for goods. This trend will probably materialize for organizations that are small or medium in size sooner than it materializes for large organizations due to the large organizations' buying power.

Firm Pricing. Firm pricing (fixed pricing) might take one of the following formats:

- Firm pricing with no variability.
  - *Description:* Vendor will charge your organization a firm price for goods or services during the contract.
  - *Example:* Hotel contract where your organization pays for X number of rooms at Y rate per room, per night.
  - *Audit considerations:* Be sure to use the vendor's pro forma invoice to describe the goods or services in your contract. This will help ensure that the goods or services listed on an invoice match the contract.
  - *How a vendor might try to take advantage of your organization:* A vendor might try a "bait and switch" tactic where the contract pricing is for a specific good or service but then tell end users within your organization that the specific good or service is no longer available and only higher-priced options are available.

    An example of this would be where Ultimate Skills Assessment Corporation (USAC) offers various tests to allow a library to offer skill assessments to its patrons. USAC's contract has a stated price list that references specific SKU numbers for stated tests. USAC is a very shady company, and they often discontinue tests without providing advanced notice, change the SKU number to something not stated in the contract, and charge much more than the contract rate.
  - *How to mitigate risk:*
    - In the contract, state that the vendor must not sell any goods or services to your organization unless the exact good or service is listed in the contract between your organization and the vendor.
    - Ensure that someone at your organization keeps the contract and its price lists current.
    - Ensure that someone at your organization is monitoring the vendor on a routine basis to ensure that the vendor complies with the contract.
- Price based on an objective index.
  - *Description:* Vendor will charge your organization based on an objective price index published by a third party. Usually, the vendor will charge the index price plus a certain percentage.
  - *Example:* Your organization buys gasoline, which is often priced at the Oil Price Information Service (OPIS)[20] Index plus a certain percentage.
  - *Audit considerations:* Does your organization have access to the index? And does the index publish previous/historical data?
  - *How a vendor might try to take advantage of your organization:* The vendor might "accidentally" charge a higher percentage than the contract

rate. If the vendor was supposed to charge index plus 4%, the vendor might try index plus 4.5%.

- *How to mitigate risk:* Be sure to monitor the vendor's invoices and determine whether the vendor charged your organization the correct costs.

- Firm pricing with escalator clause.

- *Example:* Your organization signs a five-year contract with a publishing company for a journal package, and the publisher will charge $400,000 per year for the first year, with each subsequent year's cost increasing by 5%.

- Firm pricing with vendor retaining right to adjust pricing in the future (but the adjustment isn't capped or otherwise tied to an objective standard).

- *Example:* Paper Clips, Inc., is a national office supplies seller, and Paper Clips' contract allows for Paper Clips to increase its pricing once per year at an uncertain rate. Paper Clips will provide letters from its vendors justifying the cost increases.

Think carefully when you structure a service contract with hourly rates. Allowing the vendor to charge your organization by the hour could, in certain circumstances, provide the vendor with an incentive to complete the work slowly. Thus, the vendor can ensure higher revenue. With painting, landscaping, etc., consider other pricing options, such as per-job, per-square-foot, or similar pricing alternatives.

Discount Pricing. Many procurement offices, especially government procurement offices, still maintain firm pricing as their primary model. Although firm pricing is much easier to verify, it can result in overpayment. The world's markets move very fast, and pricing often changes daily for some goods. A discount-based pricing model might help your organization achieve better pricing in terms of market reasonableness, but discount pricing can be difficult to manage and hard to audit.

Pricing models based on discounts will likely follow one of the following common formats:

- Discount off manufacturer's suggested retail price (MSRP):
  - *Description:* A discount off an MSRP.
  - *Example:* Acme Cartoon Widgets offers 15% off MSRP for Lucy's Best Chocolate.
  - *Audit considerations:* You must be able to verify the MSRP by reaching out to the manufacturer directly.
  - *How a vendor might try to take advantage of your organization:*
    - Manufacturers might maintain multiple MSRP lists for different sectors (government, other nonprofit, private-sector companies, etc.).
    - The vendor most likely does not pay MSRP and might be paying substantially less. Moreover, sometimes manufacturers issue rebates and other incentives to their resellers/distributors.

- ○ *How to mitigate risk:*
  - Ensure that you have access to MSRP, including future updates to the MSRP.
  - Include language in your contract that the vendor cannot raise its pricing without providing you with proof from the manufacturer that the manufacturer is raising the MSRP.
- Discount off vendor's website: This pricing model is not very common, but it is worth seeking. This pricing model is particularly useful when the vendor has a website through which it sells its entire catalog to the public. The idea is that using the vendor's public website pricing as the baseline ensures that your organization always gets better pricing than the public.
  - ○ *Description:* Vendor applies a general discount to the price listed on the vendor's website for all items.
  - ○ *Example:* Twelve percent discount on writing utensils applied to the vendor's public website price for all writing utensils.
  - ○ *Audit considerations:*
    - What will happen if the vendor's public website offers a sale?
    - How will you be able to retroactively audit? It's easy to audit in real time: compare the public price to the price the vendor is offering your organization through your organization's ordering platform when using this pricing model. However, comparing the price your organization paid on an invoice to the price that your organization should have been charged on the day your organization ordered the item can be challenging.
  - ○ *How a vendor might try to take advantage of your organization:* As long as the vendor actually applies the discounts, the vendor's pricing will always be correct. This is the safest pricing model to use, but it's a pricing model that many vendors do not offer as of the date of this writing.
  - ○ *How to mitigate risk:* Do frequent audits to ensure that the vendor is charging your organization correctly.
- Discount off list: Discounts off a price list are one of the most common pricing models that vendors offer. This pricing model brings many challenges, though. The biggest concerns are:
  - ○ Does the vendor maintain multiple lists?
  - ○ How often does the list price change?
  - ○ Will you be notified of list price changes?

When considering pricing models, please remember that the ultimate goal is to ensure that the vendor's pricing is 100% transparent and easy to verify/audit.

With any discount-based pricing model, if the discount varies by category, it is critical that you think through how the vendor's goods or services will be categorized. For example, consider a contract that a university has with a vendor who sells general science and laboratory supplies. If the vendor has a category for "equipment" and a category for "instruments," in which category does a microscope fall? Consider, also, whether the vendor will have the ability to switch an item from one category to another (a likely scenario if the vendor's marketing team can control how items are categorized). Some questions to consider:

- How will you be able to know in which category an item belongs?
- Will the category appear on the vendor's invoices?
- How will the vendor categorize new items?
- What happens when a vendor sells discontinued items?
- Does the vendor sell used items, including refurbished items? If so, how are those classified?
- How will the vendor price customized (custom-built) items?
- How will the vendor price configurable items?

The authors have no easy answers to these issues. In our experience, very few contract professionals dig this deep into pricing models with vendors. Therefore, vendors are accustomed to offering what appears to be a transparent deal, but the deal is often not transparent. Rather, the deal allows the vendor flexibility to adjust pricing in a manner that best suits the vendor. In our experience, some vendors fight very hard to resist providing you with price lists, product categorization, etc., citing trade secret concerns.

Our suggestion is that you explore these issues with your vendors and make as much progress as the vendor will allow. Common challenges with discount-based pricing include:

- Vendor offers pricing based on discounts from a price list, but the vendor refuses to provide the price list.
- Vendor offers discounts that vary based on category, but the vendor does not provide a way for your organization to categorize the items you buy.
- Vendor offers items that are not included in its price lists.
- Vendor changes its price list often.

Cost Plus. Generally, cost-plus pricing is a suboptimal pricing model to use because the vendor has no incentive to reduce its costs. For example, if the vendor's pricing model is cost plus 20%, then the vendor makes more money if the vendor's costs are higher. If possible, try to avoid cost-plus pricing models because of the vendor's incentive to increase their costs. Another consideration is that large vendors often get rebates and other incentives from the vendors they buy from. This is relevant because a vendor might buy Widget X from a vendor and then produce documentation to your organization showing where the vendor paid $5,000 for Widget X. It is possible that the vendor buys extremely large quantities of Widget X and gets a 5% rebate from its vendor. So, the vendor's cost is not exactly what the vendor claims.

When encountering cost-plus pricing, there are generally two types of tactics that a vendor might offer: cost plus fixed fee and cost plus percentage. Cost plus fixed fee is less risky because the vendor's costs will not drive the upcharge rate. Note that cost plus percentage is a common pricing model in certain market sectors, so you might not be able to avoid cost plus percentage pricing.

In some cases, cost-plus pricing might end up yielding the best price for your organization. In cases where the vendor's costs vary based on order size, a discount-based pricing model would yield a worse price outcome than a cost-plus model at some point once the order size reached a certain level. Consider accounting for this scenario in discount-based pricing models. You could consider negotiating additional discounts once order sizes reached a certain threshold.

Time and Materials. Time and materials can be thought of as a hybrid pricing arrangement where the vendor charges a fixed fee for hourly labor rates and adds cost-plus pricing for materials. Time and materials is a common pricing model for construction, maintenance, consultants, and similar services.

Under a time-and-materials cost model, the vendor charges your organization at a mutually agreed hourly rate plus the vendor's costs for its materials. The vendor will often add a markup to its cost for materials, and sometimes a vendor will add a service charge on top of the materials cost with markup (in that case, the vendor is charging your organization a fee for buying the items it needs to fulfill its end of the contract).

Vendors will often charge different hourly rates based on the skill level of its staff members who perform work. For example, the vendor might charge $100/hour for a technician and $250/hour for a manager.

You will need to require the vendor to provide you with proof of their costs. Consider how much detail you need to require the vendor to provide. If the vendor buys items at Walmart, Lowe's, Home Depot, or many other major stores, many of the receipts from such stores provide almost no detail as to what the vendor bought—for example, a vendor might buy lighting and electrical materials but also buy sodas and candy bars. It will be difficult for you to identify the fraudulent charges based on the generic details from the receipts. Also, a vendor might buy something that the vendor can use in the future, a durable item, such as a hammer, drill, or pair of boots. If the vendor buys durable goods, consider whether the vendor will need to leave the durable goods with you after completing their work. If not, then your organization does not need to pay for the full cost of the durable goods that the vendor will keep.

Conducting frequent, random audits is the best way to monitor time-and-materials–based contracts.

Rebates and Signing Bonuses. Many vendors offer a rebate or signing bonus to incentivize your organization to use the vendor. Signing bonuses are the easiest and most transparent incentive because your organization knows the amount it will receive at the time you sign the contract with the vendor. When considering a signing bonus, think about:

- When will the vendor pay the bonus?
- How will the vendor pay the bonus?
- When does your organization earn the bonus?
- What happens if either party terminates the contract early?

Rebates merit more thought. Rebates will take one of the following forms:

- Firm rebate
- Rebate tiers based on spend amounts
- Rebates tied to metrics

With all rebates, consider whether the vendor will be able to capture 100% of your organization's spend, regardless of whether the spending comes from procurement cards or direct bill/invoice.

- Firm rebate:
  - *Description:* Vendor will provide your organization a rebate based on every dollar that your organization spends. The rebate will be a firm/flat percentage.
  - *Example:* A 2.5% rebate for all of your organization's spending with the vendor.
  - *Audit considerations:* Your organization will need to be able to verify its spending against the vendor's records.
  - *How a vendor might try to take advantage of your organization:* Vendor might fail to capture all of your organization's spending.
  - *How to mitigate risk:* In your contract, be sure to define what counts as a sale for purposes of the rebate. Require the vendor to provide you with advanced notice of the rebate payments to give you a chance to verify the amount. Please note that your organization's spending records and the vendor's sales records to your organization will never match exactly. These two sets of data will vary based on payment terms, returns/refunds, and other factors.
- Rebate tiers based on spending:
  - *Description:* Vendor's rebate is based on tiers/levels of your organization's spending.

- *Example:* Acme Company offers your organization a rebate tier as follows:

  Spending in a given contract year:
  - $0 to $500,000: no rebate
  - $500,000.01 to $999,999.99: 1%
  - $1,000,000 to $1,999,999.99: 2%, etc.
- *Audit considerations:*
  - Your organization will need to be able to verify its spending against the vendor's records.
  - Time will play a role (possibly a big role) in which tier your organization hits. Will the vendor use invoice date, order date, or the date the vendor deposits the revenue to count the spending in a given contract year?
- *How a vendor might try to take advantage of your organization:* The vendor might "play games" with its accounts receivable. If the vendor sees that you are going to place a very large order toward the end of the contract year, then the vendor might be slow to invoice, slow to receive the order, or slow to recognize the revenue.
- *How to mitigate risk:*
  - Be sure to define carefully when the vendor will count spending toward your organization's spending tier.
  - In your contract, be sure to define what counts as a sale for purposes of the rebate. Require the vendor to provide you with advanced notice of the rebate payments to give you a chance to verify the amount. Please note that your organization's spending records and the vendor's sales records to your organization will never match exactly. These two sets of data will vary based on payment terms, returns/refunds, and other factors.

- Rebate based on metrics:
  - *Description:* Vendor will pay your organization a rebate if your organization reaches certain metrics.
  - *Example:* Vendor will pay a rebate to your organization if your organization maintains an average order size of $500 per order.
  - *Audit considerations:* How much control over order size, or the relevant metric, does your organization have? Are there steps you can take to improve the odds that your organization will reach the metric?
  - *How a vendor might try to take advantage of your organization:* The vendor might not capture all spending from your organization. For example, the vendor might not count orders from your organization toward your organization's total order count unless the person placing the order identifies themselves as being from your organization.
  - *How to mitigate risk:*
    - Be sure to provide your organization with the ability to track the metrics independently of the vendor's calculations.

- Take all reasonable steps to increase the odds that your organization will reach the vendor's minimum metrics.
  - Ensure that the vendor captures 100% of orders from your organization, or at least the vendor makes a good-faith effort to capture as close to 100% as possible.
- In your contract, be sure to define what counts as a sale for purposes of the rebate. Require the vendor to provide you with advanced notice of the rebate payments to give you a chance to verify the amount. Please note that your organization's spending records and the vendor's sales records to your organization will never match exactly. These two sets of data will vary based on payment terms, returns/refunds, and other factors.

Rebates are a common feature in high-volume contracts for goods, such as office supplies. Contracts involving rebates require careful thought to ensure that you consider all possible issues that might create problems during the life of the agreement.

Calculating the Rebate. Calculating the rebate involves considering two issues: 1) determining when the supplier will recognize your organization's spending and 2) determining how the supplier will calculate the rebate. Will the supplier count your organization's spending when:

- Your organization places an order?
- Supplier ships the item(s)?
- Your organization issues payment?
- Your organization's payment clears?
- Some other time?

The timing could make a big difference, especially when the rebate is based on tiers of spending in a given period. For example, assume the rebate is based on a calendar year and the supplier pays a rebate based on tiers of spending. If your organization places a large order on the last working day of December that would put your spending in a higher tier but the supplier doesn't fulfill the order until mid-January, when will the order count? If you fail to address this in the contract, the supplier will have control over when to count your organization's spending under the contract for purposes of calculating the rebate.

The supplier could use one of the following methods to calculate the amount of the rebate:

- *Flat percentage:* The simplest form of rebate is when the supplier will give your organization a firm rebate (for example, 1.5%) on all of your organization's spending.

- *Tiers:* If the rebate will be based on tiers, you must specify whether the rebate will go to the first dollar that your organization spends (often called "dollar one") or whether the tier structure will govern payout. An example will make this point clearer. Consider the following: your organization spends $6,000,000 with the vendor.

Tiers	Rebate Percentage
$.01 to $1,000,000.00	1%
$1,000,000.01 to $5,000,000.00	2%
$5,000,000.01 and above	3%

Tier structure applies:
$$\$1,000,000 \times .01 = \$10,000$$
$$\$3,999,999.99 \times .02 = \$79,999.99$$
$$\$999,999.99 \times .03 = \$29,999.99$$
$$\text{Total} = \$119,999.98$$

From dollar one:
$$\$6,000,000 \times .03 = \$180,000.00$$

The difference between a "dollar one" approach and the tier structure is $60,000.02.

Time and Method of Payment. What is the time period during which your organization's spending will count toward the rebate? Be sure to define whether the period is based on the calendar year or contract year. If the supplier will pay your organization a rebate based on tiers, consider whether it would be better for your organization if the supplier paid the rebate annually. Most likely, an annual rebate would be better for your organization because it would be easier for your organization to hit a higher tier over the course of a year, instead of a shorter time frame.

Another item to consider is when the supplier will pay your organization. Will payment be quarterly, annually, etc.? The best practice would be to set a certain date when the supplier will pay your organization. For example, "Supplier will pay the University no later than January 15. If January 15 is not a business day, Supplier will pay the University no later than the first business day after January 15."

How will the supplier pay your organization? Does your organization prefer a check, ACH, wire, etc.?

Note: There are other types of pricing models, but those other types are not going to arise very often for most organizations. Several U.S. federal government agencies have excellent guidelines and recommendations on cost models. For more information, please see https://www.acquisition.gov.

CONCLUSION

Understanding the basics of each transaction is critical to managing your contracts optimally. In most cases, utilizing a contract-management system can also improve your contract review. In the next chapter, we will discuss the basic clauses that appear in contracts, such as governing law.

NOTES

1. Cornell Law School, Legal Information Institute, "Sovereign Immunity," https://www.law.cornell.edu/wex/sovereign_immunity (cited March 4, 2019).
2. Issuetrak Blog, "What Are Email Tokens and Why Would You Use Them?," https://blog.issuetrak.com/what-are-email-tokens-and-why-would-you-use -them (cited March 4, 2019).
3. Stark, Tina L., *Drafting Contracts: How and Why Lawyers Do What They Do* (2nd ed.), New York: Wolters Kluwer Law & Business, 2014, p. 67.
4. Adams, Kenneth A., *A Manual of Style for Contract Drafting* (4th ed.), Chicago, IL: American Bar Association, Business Law Section, 2017, pp. 508–513, Appendix B.
5. Adams, *A Manual of Style for Contract Drafting*, p. 30, section 2.124.
6. Adams, Kenneth A., *A Manual of Style for Contract Drafting*, p. 30, section 2.129.
7. Adams, Kenneth A., *A Manual of Style for Contract Drafting*, p. 30, section 2.129.
8. Adams, Kenneth A., *A Manual of Style for Contract Drafting*, pp. 30–31, sections 2.131–2.133.
9. Adams, Kenneth A., *A Manual of Style for Contract Drafting*, p. 34, section 2.154.
10. Adams, Kenneth A., *A Manual of Style for Contract Drafting*, p. 34, sections 2.154–2.155
11. The authors' example deviates from MSCD. See MSCD, pp. 30–35, sections 2.129–2.159.
12. Adams, Kenneth A., *A Manual of Style for Contract Drafting*, pp. 245–246, section 10.52.
13. Adams, Kenneth A., *A Manual of Style for Contract Drafting*, p. 246, section 10.53.
14. Adams, Kenneth A., *A Manual of Style for Contract Drafting*, p. 246, section 10.55.
15. This list is not exhaustive.
16. Reynolds, Frank, *INCOTERMS® for Americans®: Completely Rewritten for Incoterms® 2010: Simplifies and Answers Questions About Incoterms® 2010 Rules for U.S. Business*, Toledo, OH: International Projects, 2010, p. 20.
17. Incoterms is a registered trademark of the International Chamber of Commerce (ICC). Incoterms stands for "international commercial terms." The International Chamber of Commerce owns copyright in the Incoterms. The ICC changes the Incoterms every 10 years. For more information, see the ICC's website: https://iccwbo.org/resources-for-business/incoterms-rules.

18. For a brief but very well-written summary of a commentator's opinion as to why attorneys are often poor businesspeople, please see: Barnes, Harrison. "Why Attorneys Often Fail as Businesspeople and Entrepreneurs." BCGSearch .com, https://www.bcgsearch.com/article/900047997/Why-Attorneys-Often -Fail-as-Businesspeople-and-Entrepreneurs (cited March 4, 2019).
19. Lean Enterprise Institute, "Standardized Work: The Foundation for Kaizen." https://www.lean.org/Workshops/WorkshopDescription.cfm?WorkshopId =20 (cited March 4, 2019).
20. See https://www.opisnet.com

Organizing Contracts*

INTRODUCTION

In this chapter, we continue looking at the basic building blocks of contract language. In particular, we explore common contract clauses—clauses that appear in almost all types of contracts, or at least those clauses that are likely to appear in most types of contracts.

Before doing this, we address clauses that are common to library license agreements and library subscriptions.

TERMS COMMON IN LIBRARY LICENSES AND SUBSCRIPTIONS

Access and Authentication

When applicable, language should be included that allows users to access materials remotely. Currently, this most commonly occurs via proxy/Internet Protocol (IP) authentication. However, we recommend including language that also allows the parties flexibility in using emerging authentication methods.

Example language:
Remote access will be provided to Authorized Users through the use of a secured network with IP authentication. An updated list of IP ranges will be supplied on an as-needed basis. Parties agree to cooperate in the implementation of

---

*Parts of this chapter are based on Halaychik, Corey S. and Blake Reagan, "Library Process Improvement Considerations," in *Licensing Electronic Resources in Academic Libraries: A Practical Handbook,* Cambridge, MA, and Kidlington, UK: Chandos Publishing, 2018, https://doi.org/10.1016/B978-0-08-102107-1.00007-8

new authentication methods as they are developed during the term of this Agreement.

Accessibility

Certain federal or state laws govern accessibility standards. Libraries should make efforts to include language that requires vendors to ensure their products comply with applicable laws.

Example language:
For web-based technology, Licensor must ensure that products provided under this Agreement conform to the W3C Web Content Accessibility Guidelines, version 2.0 (WCAG 2.0) at conformance levels A and AA. In the event products provided under this Agreement do not fully conform to WCAG 2.0 A and AA, Licensor must advise Licensee in writing of the nonconformance and must provide detailed information regarding the plans to achieve conformance, including but not limited to an intended timeline.

For non–web-based electronic and information technology (EIT), Licensor warrants that the products or services to be provided under this contract comply with the accessibility requirements of Section 508 of the Rehabilitation Act of 1973, as amended (29 U.S.C. 794d), and its implementing regulations set forth at Title 36, Code of Federal Regulations, Part 1194. Licensor agrees to promptly respond to and resolve any complaint regarding accessibility of its products or services.

Licensor further agrees to indemnify and hold harmless Licensee from any claims arising out of its failure to comply with the aforesaid requirements.

Failure to comply with these requirements might constitute a breach and be grounds for termination of the agreement.

Archiving and Preservation

Libraries regularly purchase materials that include options for the archiving and preservation of electronic materials. In the past, this included libraries receiving hard drives containing copies of journals, data sets, and so on. More commonly today, contracts include clauses allowing for the archival of materials in cloud-based or closed servers. Libraries must seek to establish clear requirements for the archival and preservation of electronic materials with perpetual access. This includes considering which format is preferred (physical or virtual), establishing usage rights to the archived materials, and outlining, when applicable, any costs for maintaining access remotely.

Example language:
Providing that full payment is made, the Licensor will provide the Licensee with, or the Licensee may create a copy of, the entire set of Licensed materials. The copy must be provided without any digital rights management restrictions and in an agreed-upon medium suitable to the content. The content of

the annual archive may also be made available for download/retrieval via other means as mutually agreed upon by the parties, including use of a third-party archiving service. Licensee is authorized to make further copies in perpetuity as it may deem necessary for purposes of archival preservation, refreshing, or migration, including migration to other formats, so long as the purpose of such copying is solely for continued use and/or archival retention of the data and does not violate or extend the use rights contained in this agreement. In the event the Licensor discontinues or suspends selling or licensing the Licensed Materials, the Licensee may use such archived Licensed Materials under the same terms as this Agreement.

Consortia Purchases

Libraries can see significant savings when purchasing materials as part of a consortia effort. Many libraries are members of multiple consortia, however, and it can therefore be beneficial to include language that allows a library to always take advantage of consortia pricing. Generally, this is not an issue when orders are placed via the consortium and a consortium license is in place. However, it can prove problematic when an order is placed via the consortium but the license is in place with the product's supplier instead, or in instances where organizations cannot legally allow third parties (such as a consortia) to agree to licensing terms on their behalf.

Example language:
Licensee will be eligible for any applicable discounts for orders placed via eligible consortia.

Copyright

Watch for language that requires the library to agree to requirements that are more restrictive than existing copyright law of the country in which it is based or that requires the library to agree to foreign copyright law.

Example language:
Example 1: Licensee and Authorized Users may make all use of the licensed materials as is consistent with [your country's] Copyright Law.
Example 2: Nothing in this agreement will limit either party's rights under [your country's] Copyright Law.

Course Packs/Electronic Reserves/Virtual Learning Environments

Course packs and electronic reserves are collections of materials assembled by academic libraries for the purpose of instruction. These materials allow users to easily access compilations of material without locating sources on their own. Libraries should, when appropriate, include language to allow the widest possible dissemination of information and assist instructors to share material with students.

Example language:
The Licensee may incorporate parts of the Licensed Materials in printed Course Packs, Electronic Reserve collections, and in virtual learning environments for use by Authorized Users only. Each such item incorporated will carry appropriate acknowledgement of the source, title, author of the extract, and the name of the Publisher. Course packs in nonelectronic nonprint perceptible form, such as audio or Braille, may also be offered by the Licensee to Authorized Users.

Geographical/Institution/Unified Campus

Libraries should watch out for contract language that restricts access to a single physical address. This can be problematic in cases where a library may have multiple branches on a campus or city that share the same IP range(s).

Example language:
For sake of clarity, the parties agree that it is acceptable for any of the Licensee's locations based in the same city to use the same IP range(s).

Informing Authorized Users of Limitations

Most library contracts will include language that requires the library to ensure that authorized users are made aware of limitations on usage. Although many libraries will post a usage policy somewhere, it is near impossible to guarantee users have read, understood, and agreed to any use restrictions placed on resources. Because of this, it is recommended that libraries remove any of these clauses entirely. Or in cases where a vendor will not agree to strike the clause, edit the language so that it only requires that reasonable efforts or best efforts be made to notify authorized users of limitations.

Example language:
Licensee will use all reasonable endeavors to ensure that all Authorized Users are aware of the importance of respecting the intellectual property rights in the Licensed Materials and of the terms and conditions of this License, and must notify Authorized Users of the terms and conditions of this License and take steps to protect the Licensed Materials from use which is not expressly authorized by this License.

Interlibrary Loan

Vendors will occasionally try to prohibit interlibrary lending or restrict interlibrary lending to other libraries in a specific geographic region (i.e.,

North America). Libraries should make efforts to include, when applicable, language that allows for the lending of materials via interlibrary loan.

Example language:
As part of the practice commonly known as "interlibrary loan," deliver a reasonable number of copies of Articles (including through use of Ariel or a substantially similar interlibrary loan transmission software) to fulfill requests from noncommercial, academic libraries, provided that such practice complies with Section 108 of the U.S. Copyright Act.

Monitoring and Reporting Misuse

Watch out for language that requires the library to ensure that authorized users comply with any limitations such as copyright, interlibrary, and so on and to report any violations to the supplier. It is very difficult to monitor every patron's use and compliance with such clauses. If this clause cannot be removed entirely, it is better to establish that the library will use reasonable efforts to monitor usage and, when misuse is discovered, to report it.

Example language:
Licensee will use reasonable endeavors to monitor compliance and upon becoming aware of any unauthorized use of the Licensed Materials or other breach of this License, inform the Licensor of such unauthorized use or breach and take all reasonable and appropriate steps, including disciplinary action, both to ensure that such activity ceases and to prevent any recurrence.

Patron Record Maintenance

Libraries should never agree to clauses that require that patron records be kept full and up-to-date. Patron information maintenance is an internal policy matter, and libraries should not forfeit their ability to govern such matters. As such, any clauses requiring this should be removed from an agreement.

Return of/Destruction of Materials

Libraries should be cautious of language that requires them to ensure that all materials are returned or destroyed at the end of a subscription or when a material breach by the library has occurred. This is problematic in cases of electronic resources because it is completely possible that patrons have printed or saved copies of the material, and it would be impossible for the library to guarantee that all copies have been returned or destroyed. Libraries should insist that this type of clause be deleted from an agreement or, in cases where a vendor pushes back, include language requiring that only reasonable efforts be made.

Example language:
Example 1: On termination of this License, the Licensee shall immediately cease to distribute or make available the Licensed Materials to Authorized Users and shall make reasonable efforts to return to the Licensor or destroy all Licensed Materials locally stored in accordance with the rights granted in this License.
Example 2: The Licensee will make reasonable efforts to ensure that Authorized Users return to the Licensor or destroy all Licensed Materials locally stored in accordance with the rights granted in this License.

Supplying Patron Records

Libraries should not agree to clauses that require that full patron records be shared with suppliers upon request. In rare cases, such as using a cloud-based integrated library system (ILS), personal information may need to be shared with a supplier. In such cases, the library must ensure it retains sole ownership of the data; restricts usage of the data solely for the purpose of supplying the service; and reserves the right to access, modify, or delete the data at any time.

Example language:
Licensee retains ownership of the personal information and may, at any time during the term of this agreement, access, modify, and delete personal information that the Licensor is storing. Licensor shall not use the personal information for any purpose except to provide the services and support services to Licensee and its permitted users.

Usage Statistics

Libraries should require vendors to supply useable usage statistics about their patrons' usage of resources. Currently, the preferred format for usage statistics is modeled after the Counting Online Usage of NeTworked Electronic Resources (COUNTER) Code of Practice. Furthermore, to protect patron privacy, libraries should include language that restricts how vendors use data.

Example language:
Licensor must provide data that meets or exceeds the most recent Counting Online Usage of NeTworked Electronic Resources (COUNTER) Code of Practice Release. All usage data will include system-wide and campus-specific data tracked by IPs specific to each campus. All usage data will be compiled by the Licensor in a manner consistent with privacy and data protection laws applicable to the United States, including the anonymity of Authorized Users and the confidentiality of their searches. In the case that the Licensor assigns

its rights to another party, the Licensee shall be entitled to require the assignee to confirm that it agrees to fulfill the obligations of privacy and data protection laws herein mentioned.

Walk-In Users

Walk-in users are patrons who are not affiliated with the organization in an official capacity (employees, students, faculty, etc.) but who are physically present at the library. It is common for institutions receiving taxpayer funding to allow members of the general public to use libraries. It is therefore important that libraries not agree to definitions of authorized users that exclude walk-ins.

Example language:
Walk-ins. Patrons not affiliated with the Licensee who are physically present at the Licensee's site(s) (so-called "walk-ins").

GENERAL CLAUSES

Assignment

The purpose of an anti-assignment clause is to prevent one party (or all parties) from assigning rights or delegating duties to anyone else, including other corporations. Many contracts have anti-assignment clauses, but please carefully consider whether you need to include such a clause. If your vendor needs to assign part of the work to subcontractors, consider whether it would be better to avoid including the anti-assignment clause. Another approach would be to include the anti-assignment clause but list the allowable subcontractors.

Anti-assignment clauses are particularly important where the vendor is providing highly specialized services, such as artists, performers/speaking engagements, or similar services.

Note that many anti-assignment clauses read something like, "Neither party shall . . . ." Importantly, such an anti-assignment clause does not prohibit assignments.[1] The combination of "neither" and "shall" creates language that means that neither party has an obligation to assign.[2] If your anti-assignment clause uses the word "neither," in this context, the correct word to use is "may" instead of "shall."[3] Alternatively, you might consider using "each party shall not . . . ."[4]

Example clause:
Except with the prior written consent of the other party, each party shall not transfer, including by merger (whether that party is the surviving or disappearing entity), consolidation, dissolution, or operation of law, (1) any discretion

granted under this agreement, (2) any right to satisfy a condition under this agreement, (3) any remedy under this agreement, or (4) any obligation imposed under this agreement.[5]

Options:
- Do not include an anti-assignment clause.
- Include an anti-assignment clause with language that allows one party, or both parties, to assign to named entities or individuals.
- Include an anti-assignment clause that prohibits one party from assigning.
- Include an anti-assignment clause that prohibits both parties from assigning.

What to discuss with the vendor up front: Determine whether the vendor will need to assign any of the work to subcontractors. If so, account for this in the contract's language.

Attorneys' Fees

The purpose of an attorneys' fees clause is for the parties to reduce the risk of incurring costs related to litigating the contract. Language related to attorneys' fees might be a stand-alone clause, but most often, the clause appears as part of a broader clause related to costs. Clauses requiring one party to be responsible for the other's attorneys' fees are common. The risks with an attorneys' fees clause is that the clause exposes your organization to uncapped costs. Litigation can be very expensive, after all.

Attorneys' fees clauses are typically mutual/two-way clauses, meaning that the obligation to pay attorneys' fees could happen to either party. Contract commentator Brian Rogers, "The Contracts Guy," notes that one party might be able to negotiate a one-way attorneys' fees provision.[6]

Most attorneys' fees clauses, as well as court costs clauses, provide that the "prevailing party" will be able to recover the attorneys' fees or court costs from the nonprevailing (i.e., "losing") party. An in-depth discussion of any topic exceeds the scope of this book, but please note that there are some issues with "prevailing party." In some cases, it is clear when one party prevails. In others, it is less clear.[7]

Example clauses:
One-way: The Seller is entitled to recover, and the Buyer shall pay, all costs, expenses, and legal fees (including the fees of attorneys and persons not admitted to the bar performing services under the supervision of an attorney) incurred by the Seller in enforcing this agreement.
Mutual: If either party brings any legal action or other proceeding under this agreement, then the prevailing party is entitled to recover, and the other party shall pay, all costs, expenses, and legal fees (including the fees of attorneys and persons not admitted to the bar performing services under the supervision of

an attorney) incurred by the prevailing party in the legal action or other proceeding.

Options:
- Agree to the clause.

- Delete the clause entirely. Depending on your state's laws or organizational practices, this might be the best option for your organization, or perhaps your only option.

- Modify the language by adding "to the extent allowed by _____ [specific state, such as New York] law . . .", or perhaps "to the extent allowed by applicable law," in front of the attorneys' fees clause. This approach is common with some governmental organizations, but please be sure to consult with your attorney before using this approach. If your organization already uses this approach, be sure to consult with your attorney to determine whether this approach is one that your organization needs to continue. If state law prohibits your organization from paying attorneys' fees (which is a common restriction for state government organizations), ask your attorney whether adding the phrase "to the extent allowed by . . . law" would operate as an attempted waiver of sovereign immunity, or whether the language would unfairly give the other party the perception that your organization can actually pay attorneys' fees when, in reality, it cannot legally agree to do so.

Common questions that vendors will ask if you strike the attorneys' fees clause:
- Is there a statute that says that your organization cannot pay attorneys' fees? Note: If your organization is a state or federal government agency, your organization most likely has sovereign immunity. In that case, your organization most likely can only be sued for what statutes allow. Assuming your organization is a state government agency, your organization might have to explain to a vendor that even though there is not a statute that says something like "thou shalt not pay attorneys' fees," if the statutes waiving your organization's sovereign immunity do not allow for attorneys' fees, your organization cannot be sued for them.

- [Assuming that state law prohibits you from agreeing to pay attorneys' fees:] Can we reinsert attorneys' fees if we change the contract language to state, "To the extent allowed by [state] law . . ."? Be sure to check with your attorney on this question.

- If striking the attorneys' fees is a business issues instead of a legal one, consider your possible reasoning for striking attorneys' fees.

What to tell the vendor up front: If you modify or delete the clause, be sure to articulate the precise reason(s) why. If you can cite a state law, state attorney general opinion, or corporate resolution/official policy that prohibits your organization from paying attorneys' fees, provide a citation and copy of the law, opinion, or resolution/policy.

Automatic Renewal

Contracts almost always contain both a start date and an end date. And although some simpler contracts might not state a start and end date, the best practice is for all contracts to contain one of each. Many service agreements, including subscription agreements, contain a clause where the vendor seeks to have the contract automatically renew after the initial term expires.

Many companies want to reduce paperwork and help stabilize their future income, so many contracts will include language stating that the contract automatically renews unless the other party provides notice of its intent not to renew within a specified period. Often, the period is very long, such as requiring your institution to provide the vendor with no less than 180 days before the end of the then-current term.

Not only do many automatic renewal clauses require your institution to submit notice of termination/nonrenewal many months in advance, it is very common for automatic renewal clauses to automatically renew the contract for a long period, such as three to five years.

Another issue that arises with automatic renewal clauses is how will your organization account for the automatic renewal in your organization's contract-management software? The best-case scenario would be if your organization could store the following data: (a) that the agreement automatically renews, (b) the deadline to stop automatic renewal, and (c) the end date if the automatic renewal is cancelled. Further, the optimal situation is if your contract-management software could provide notice, or multiple notices, automatically via email some period in advance before the deadline to stop automatic renewal passes. For example, the contract-management software emails the appropriate organization staff 60, 45, and 30 days in advance. While multiple emails might sound annoying, many people tend to lose emails, and the multiple notifications help offset the odds that someone overlooks them.

In the authors' experience, automatic renewal clauses are among the highest-risk clauses and are very likely to cause real-world problems. In one example, a department had to pay $12,000 for a software product that it did not want because a contract review staff member failed to strike an automatic renewal clause.

There was no "happy ending" to that situation. The department ended up asking the vendor to cancel without penalty, and the university involved had to admit that one of its contract review staff members made a mistake by not striking the clause. If the university's contract review staff member had noticed the clause before the university's authorized official signed the contract, the university would have been in a stronger bargaining position (i.e., had some leverage) to negotiate the clause. Because the issue arose after both parties signed the contract, the university had no leverage and was forced to beg (instead of negotiate). The vendor ended up allowing the university to terminate the contract early, provided that the university paid a reduced rate as a cancellation fee ($12,000 instead of $18,000). So, in the end, no one was happy: the vendor was upset because they saw the university as revoking on a promise to pay for the automatically renewed term, and the department was unhappy because they had to pay for a product they did not want.

Example clause:
Unless Customer provides notice of non-renewal at least 180 days before this agreement's end date, this agreement will automatically renew for a five-year term.

Things to consider:
- Does your organization's policies, rules, and so on allow it to agree to automatic renewal provisions?
- Does your state have laws that limit your organization's ability to agree to automatic renewal clauses?
- Does your organization have the ability to track automatic renewal clauses? If not, then the best practice would be to never agree to automatic renewal clauses.

Options:
- Agree to the automatic renewal clause, despite its practical risks.
- Negotiate a shorter notice period. For example, provide that your organization may stop the automatic renewal by giving notice no less than 30 days before the scheduled renewal date.
- Negotiate a shorter automatic renewal period. For example, provide that the automatic renewal period is one year, or perhaps even shorter. Automatic renewal would be much lower risk where the automatically renewed term is month to month.
- Delete the clause entirely.

Collection Costs

Collection costs are costs associated with collecting debt owed to one party. When the customer is late with payment and the seller has not been able to collect from the buyer through normal efforts (e.g., sending invoices, etc.), the seller might engage a collection company. Similar to attorneys' fees, collection costs potentially expose your organization to uncapped costs.

Initially, you might think that it will be unlikely that your organization will be late on payment and thus there's little risk in agreeing to a collection costs clause. Making that assumption could be very risky. If your organization allows end users to have procurement cards, those purchases might increase the odds that your organization pays late. Here's how: Assume the vendor does not charge the end user's procurement card until the vendor ships an item. Assume that the end user places an order and the vendor cannot fulfill the order for several weeks. Sometime before the vendor fulfills the order, the end user leaves the organization. If the organization closes the procurement card account, it is unlikely that the organization will know about the pending order. The vendor might fulfill the order even if the procurement card transaction fails. If the vendor emails an invoice to the departed staff member and the staff member does not forward the invoice, your organization is likely going to fall behind on making this payment.

If your organization does not have centralized accounts payable, consider whether you want to provide your vendors with a central point of contact for the vendor to contact in the event of late payment. The best practice would be to set a group email address as the point of contact—for example, ap@organization.edu. Consider, also, whether you want to require vendors to attempt to contact the central point of contact before being able to seek collection costs.

Options:
- Agree to the clause.
- Delete the clause entirely. Depending on your state's laws or organizational practices, this might be the best option for your organization, or perhaps your only option.
- Modify the language by adding "to the extent allowed by _____ [specific state, such as New York] law . . .", or perhaps "to the extent allowed by applicable law," in front of the collection costs clause. This approach is common with some governmental organizations, but please be sure to consult with your attorney before using this approach. If your organization already uses this approach, be sure to consult with your attorney to determine whether this is an approach that your organization needs to continue. If state law prohibits your organization from paying collection costs (which is a common restriction for state government organizations), ask your attorney whether adding the phrase "to the extent allowed by . . . law" would operate as an attempted waiver of sovereign immunity, or whether the language would unfairly give the other party the perception that your organization can actually pay collection costs when, in reality, it cannot legally agree to do so.

Common questions that vendors will ask if you strike the collection costs clause:
- Is there a statute that says your organization cannot pay collection costs? Note: If your organization is a state or federal government agency, your organization most likely has sovereign immunity. In that case, your organization most likely can only be sued for what statutes allow. Assuming your organization is a state government agency, your organization might have to explain to a vendor that even though there is not a statute that says something like "thou shalt not pay

collection costs," if the statutes waiving your organization's sovereign immunity do not allow for collection costs, your organization cannot be sued for them. Please be sure to consult with your legal counsel.

- [Assuming that state law prohibits you from agreeing to pay collection costs:] Can we reinsert the collection costs language if we change the contract language to state, "To the extent allowed by [state] law . . ."? Be sure to check with your attorney on this question.
- If striking the collection costs is a business issue instead of a legal one, consider your possible reasoning for striking this clause.

What to tell the vendor up front: If you modify or delete the clause, be sure to articulate the precise reason(s) why. If you can cite a state law, state attorney general opinion, or corporate resolution/official policy that prohibits your organization from paying collection costs, provide a citation and copy of the law, opinion, or resolution/policy.

Court Costs

Court costs are typically not anywhere as expensive as attorneys' fees, but many contract parties seek to shift court costs to the nonprevailing party. Such clauses are common. Many government agencies are not able to pay for another party's court costs per state law.

Example clause (the language used in the attorneys' fees section works for court costs too, because the language accounts for "all costs, expenses . . ."): If either party brings any legal action or other proceeding under this agreement, then the prevailing party is entitled to recover, and the other party shall pay, all costs, expenses, and legal fees (including the fees of attorneys and persons not admitted to the bar performing services under the supervision of an attorney) incurred by the prevailing party in the legal action or other proceeding.

Options:
- Agree to the clause.
- Delete the clause entirely. Depending on your state's laws or organizational practices, this might be the best option for your organization, or perhaps your only option.
- Modify the language by adding "to the extent allowed by _____ [specific state, such as New York] law . . .", or perhaps "to the extent allowed by applicable law," in front of the court costs clause. This approach is common with some governmental organizations, but please be sure to consult with your attorney before using this approach. If your organization already uses this approach, be sure to consult with your attorney to determine whether this is an approach that your organization needs to continue. If state law prohibits your organization from paying court costs (which is a common restriction for state government organizations), ask your attorney whether adding the phrase "to the extent allowed by . . . law" would operate as an

attempted waiver of sovereign immunity, or whether the language would unfairly give the other party the perception that your organization can actually pay court costs when, in reality, it cannot legally agree to do so.

Counterparts

Counterparts clauses allow the parties to sign in different locations, at different times, or even to sign separate copies of the same document, and the clause expresses the parties' intent that the copy either party signed may be used as an original. This clause is useful in case of litigation, where one party (or both) will need to produce a copy of the original contract for evidence purposes.[8]

Model language:
If the parties sign this agreement in several counterparts, each will be deemed an original but all counterparts together will constitute one instrument.

Dispute Resolution

Alternative dispute resolution (ADR) refers to methods attorneys use to settle disputes other than traditional litigation. Reasons for pursuing ADR vary, but are usually based on the notion that ADR is less expensive and less time consuming than traditional litigation. Generally, there are three types of ADR:

1. Arbitration
   a. Binding
   b. Nonbinding
2. Mediation
3. Negotiation between high-ranking officials

ADR must never be a prerequisite to a lawsuit. You must ensure that contract language allowing ADR does not require ADR to occur before either party may file a claim against the other.

Arbitration. In arbitration, a neutral person called an "arbitrator" hears arguments and evidence from each side and then decides the outcome of the dispute. Arbitration may be either "binding" or "nonbinding."[9] There are two key considerations for arbitration clauses: Is your organization allowed to agree to arbitration? And is your organization willing (as a business matter) to resolve disputes via arbitration?

Fix:
- *Preferred*: Delete the clause entirely.
- *Alternative*: Suggest that the dispute resolution clause be changed to informal negotiation or voluntary mediation.

Mediation. In mediation, an impartial person called a "mediator" helps the parties try to reach a mutually acceptable resolution of the dispute. The mediator does not decide the dispute, but instead helps the parties communicate so they can try to settle the dispute themselves. Mediation leaves control of the outcome with the parties.

Mediation might be acceptable to your organization. When considering a mediation clause, consider the following:

- Whether mediation is optional or mandatory.
  - If it is mandatory, is it a necessary step that the parties must complete before moving forward to a lawsuit? In other words, must the parties go through mediation before they can file a lawsuit?
  - If it is optional, which party may invoke the option? Only one or both? If both, what happens if one doesn't agree?
- Where will mediation take place?
- When will mediation take place?
- Who will pay for the mediator?
- What qualifications must the mediator have?

Negotiation between High-Ranking Officials. Simply out, this involves high-level officials from each party (or all parties) negotiating in an attempt to avoid a lawsuit. This simple technique is not a formal alternative dispute resolution mechanism, but it is a form of alternative dispute resolution. This option might be worth considering as a way to avoid litigation. If your organization favors this method as a dispute resolution mechanism, consider whether you want to add a clause requiring that the parties attempt to negotiate their dispute before either party may file a lawsuit.

Entire Agreement (Merger or Integration)

The entire agreement clause is also known as a "merger clause," an "integration clause," or a "zipper clause."[10] The purpose of this clause is to prevent the parties from allowing items outside of the contract itself to inform a court of the parties' intent. Although courts are sometimes unpredictable,[11] they typically will enforce a merger clause.[12] Generally speaking, all of your organization's contracts need to include a merger clause.

Example clause:
This agreement constitutes the entire understanding between the parties with respect to the subject matter of this agreement and supersedes all other agreements, whether written or oral, between the parties.

The prevalence of online terms merits discussion. Many suppliers apparently do not think through the issue of whether the supplier's online terms conflict with the supplier's contract terms. To be safe, consider whether you want to add language clearly stating that the supplier's online terms do not apply to the transaction. A few risks are involved when the supplier has online terms:

- The online terms might conflict with the contract(s) between your organization and the supplier.
- The supplier can change their online terms at any time.
- Who within your organization might be clicking to accept the online terms?

The issue notes earlier goes beyond online terms. Many suppliers also include terms on their invoices, packaging, and so on. Another consideration is this: What happens if your supplier is a reseller or distributor and the original equipment manufacturer includes terms on its website, packaging, or other places? Be sure to think through these issues carefully.

Model language:
In the event that Supplier's website, mobile applications, or other platforms contain click-wrap, browse-wrap, or shrink-wrap terms and conditions, Supplier states that such terms do not apply to Customer.

Exclusivity

An exclusivity clause is a clause where the parties agree that the buyer will transact exclusively with the seller. Exclusivity obligations can be narrow in scope, such as with a requirements clause for one particular good, or an exclusivity obligation can be very broad in scope, such as an athletic sponsorship agreement. If a contract contains an exclusivity obligation, you must make the obligation as narrow as possible and as clear and specific as possible. Exclusivity obligations are common in the following scenarios:

- Athletic food or beverage vendors
- Athletic sponsorships
- Copy or print managed services
- Managed services for premium seating or special events, such as catering for skyboxes
- Media rights agreements for athletic events, logos, and other intellectual property
- Outsourced bookstore management
- Outsourced food services (e.g., contracts with companies to run cafeterias or other retail dining operations)

- Procurement card vendors
- Vending/pouring rights
- Travel agency

The organization must take its exclusivity obligations very seriously because the obligations are easy to breach, especially with large organizations. The authors suggest that your organization take a four-pronged approach to managing exclusivity obligations:

1. Assign the responsibility of monitoring and managing exclusivity obligations to one office. Assign a team within that office to manage the exclusivity obligations. Ensure that the office meets regularly to discuss upcoming renewals, expirations, and pending negotiations.

2. Ensure that the people within your organization responsible for reviewing contracts and making purchases are well trained on the issue of exclusivity. Violating an exclusivity obligation can create multiple problems for your organization.

3. Ensure that your organization has a contract-management software system that allows the contract or procurement office to tag a contract as containing an exclusivity obligation. This will allow your organization to search for all contracts that contain exclusivity obligations easily. The key is to ensure that all contract staff correctly categorize contracts with exclusivity obligations. The more decentralized your organization is with data entry, the more likely the data will contain mistakes.

4. Create a spreadsheet to manage your organization's exclusivity obligations. An example of the headers you might want to use appears in the following example. All stakeholders within the organization need real-time access to the latest version of the spreadsheet.

Contract #	Vendor Name	Vendor Number	Start Date	End Date	Category	Campus/ Unit	Page #	Brief Summary of Exclusivity Obligations

- Contract number: The number assigned by your organization's contract-management system.
- Vendor name: The vendor's legal or doing-business-as (DBA) name. Listing either is fine, but if there is a difference, ensure that you are consistent (i.e., always list the legal name or always list the DBA name).
- Vendor number: The vendor number assigned by your organization's enterprise resource planning (ERP)/accounting system.
- Start date: The start date of the contract.
- End date: The end date of the contract.

- Category: Create consistent categories for each type of contract, such as "Food Service" or "Athletic Sponsorship." Ensure that you use categories consistently, and ensure that you avoid unnecessary hyper-specificity when it comes to the categories (for example, "Athletic Sponsorship" is sufficient, whereas "Athletic Sponsorship: Football" could lead to unnecessary confusion).

- Campus/Unit (Department): Define the campus, unit, or department that is primarily responsible for the agreement.

- Page #: List the page number or numbers where the exclusivity provision appears.

- Brief Summary of Exclusivity Obligations: Describe in one to two sentences the nature of the exclusivity provision in general terms.

If your organization has multiple campuses, be sure to articulate clearly where the exclusivity applies. For example, consider the University of Cats, which has campuses in Feline City, Los Gatos, and Purrville. The university's Los Gatos football team (the Sand Cats) has an exclusive sponsorship deal with Fur Shield, a popular sports apparel and equipment company. In exchange for free products from Fur Shield, the university's football team promises to use only Fur Shield clothing and equipment. In the draft contract, the university needs to specify that the exclusivity obligation only applies to the Los Gatos campus, and further only applies to the Los Gatos football team. The university could state something like the following: "The parties acknowledge that the exclusivity obligations imposed on the University in this agreement only apply to the University's Los Gatos campus's football team."

Carefully think through purchases that might violate existing exclusivity obligations. For example, the University of Cats, Los Gatos Campus has a band that administratively reports to the Fiona College of Music. The football team administratively reports to the Department of Athletics. The College of Music and the Department of Athletics each utilize the central procurement office for the University of Cats system administration. If the band wants to order uniforms from Bite, the central procurement office must ensure that this purchase does not violate the university's agreement with Fur Shield.

Be sure to define the scope of the exclusivity obligations carefully. The vendor will want to draft the agreement as broadly as possible, whereas the organization will want to draft the agreement as narrowly as possible.

Force Majeure (Acts of God)

"Force majeure" means "superior force." In practice, a force majeure clause allows the parties to allocate the risk of one party's nonperformance due to a force majeure event.[13] A common type of force majeure clause is to include a "laundry list" of possible occurrences, such as earthquakes, war, meteor strikes, etc. The laundry-list approach requires the parties to list all possible occurrences,[14] which could lead to comically long lists. Some contract drafters have attempted to correct the issue of needing to list every possible occurrence by including catch-all language, such as "or similar cause."[15]

Another approach is to define a force majeure event by the impact on the party (or parties) affected, as opposed to defining the force majeure event by the name of the specific situation that might arise.

In addition to drafting the section as well as possible, do not rely on a (even well-drafted) force majeure clause if you are concerned about specific possible events. For example, if you book catering, hotels, equipment rental, and so on for a speaker, performer, or lecturer, what happens if the speaker, performer, or lecturer dies, becomes ill, or otherwise is unable (or unwilling) to perform? Other similar possible circumstances include a government agency (or other agency providing a grant) revoking grant funding or revising the scope of the grant funding to prohibit your organization's intended use.

One of the co-authors experienced two real-life examples of the scenarios listed here. In one instance, a relatively famous person who was under contract to speak at a university received a more lucrative offer and cancelled the booking with the university. For the purposes of this book, we will ignore the contract terms between the speaker's agent and the university. The university failed to account for this scenario in its contracts with hotels and other associated providers, so the university was left paying a significant amount of money in cancellation fees.

In another scenario, a government agency had contractually agreed to fund a grant to a university for the purposes of the university hosting a forum/conference. After the government agency and the university signed the contract, the university relied on that funding to start booking hotels, catering, audiovisual equipment, speakers, and so on for the conference. Sometime later, the "great recession" occurred, and the government agency exercised its contractual right to cancel the grant contract and thus cancel any future funding. The university was left with a $40,000 cancellation bill to hotels.

Use critical thinking and careful planning to help mitigate the risks of your organization facing a similar set of circumstances.

Sample language:[16]
12.4 Force Majeure. (a) If a Force Majeure Event prevents a party from complying with any one or more obligations under this agreement, that inability to comply will not constitute breach if (1) that party uses reasonable efforts to perform those obligations, (2) that party's inability to perform those obligations is not due to its failure to (A) take reasonable measures to protect itself against events or circumstances of the same type as that Force Majeure Event or (B) develop and maintain a reasonable contingency plan to respond to events or circumstances of the same type as that Force Majeure Event, and (3) that party complies with its obligations under Section 12.4(c).

(b) For purposes of this agreement, "**Force Majeure Event**" means, with respect to a party, any event or circumstance, whether or not foreseeable, that was not caused by that party (other than a strike or other labor unrest that affects only that party, an increase in prices or other change in general economic conditions, a change in law, or an event or circumstance that results in that party's not having sufficient funds to comply with an obligation to pay money) and any consequences of that event or circumstance.

(c) If a Force Majeure Event occurs, the noncomplying party shall promptly notify the other party of occurrence of that Force Majeure Event, its effect on performance, and how long the noncomplying party expects it to last. Thereafter, the noncomplying party shall update that information as reasonably necessary. During a Force Majeure Event, the noncomplying party shall use reasonable efforts to limit damages to the other party and to resume its performance under this agreement.

Governing Law

Governing law clauses are sometimes referred to as "choice of law" clauses. Each state's laws vary, sometimes significantly, so to help reduce uncertainty, parties often include a governing law clause in contracts. Parties to a contract usually select either governing law that benefits one of the parties over the other or governing law that is neutral. Often, government agencies are restricted in their ability to agree to governing law other than the state in which the agency is located.

Options:
1. Select the governing law that is most favorable for your organization.
2. Remain "silent" on governing law. In other words, delete the governing law clause. This approach is a common when a private-sector supplier contracts with a government agency. This approach allows the parties to move forward with their contract when governing law is an issue over which neither party will agree on a particular state's law as governing law. The downside to this approach is that remaining "silent" on governing law adds a lot of uncertainty to the contract. After all, if the parties end up litigating, they will have to file their lawsuit in a venue (usually a court, but not always; some government organizations litigate their claims in an administrative venue). That venue will select the governing law.
3. State that claims brought by the supplier against your organization will be governed by the law most favorable to your organization, but claims brought by your organization against the supplier will be governed by the supplier's preferred state's/country's laws. This approach carries some of the same risk as the "silence" approach, but this approach is an option that you and your legal counsel might want to consider. For purposes of this book, the authors will refer to this approach as a "mutual governing law."

Model language:
Governing law: The laws of the state of [state in which organization is located] (without regard to its conflict of law principles) govern all matters arising under or relating to this agreement.

Mutual governing law: All adversarial proceedings brought by [organization] against Vendor will be governed by the laws of the Netherlands (without regard to its conflict of law provisions) and will be submitted in the courts of Rotterdam. All claims brought by Vendor against [organization] will be governed by the laws of the state of Tennessee (without regard to its conflict of law provisions) and will be submitted in state courts located in Nashville, Tennessee.

Indemnification[17]

Indemnification is often expressed in contracts with three seemingly separate concepts: "indemnify, defend, and hold harmless." For purposes of this book, the authors will treat indemnification as including the duty to "hold harmless" and "defend." Whether those three items are distinct concepts or not is irrelevant for our purpose because, with careful drafting, you can address the appropriate duties involved in indemnification.[18]

Indemnification clauses shift risk of liability from one party to the other. Note that indemnification only arises when a third party makes a claim against one of the parties to a contract.[19] Generally speaking, indemnification clauses shift liability for any occurrence, regardless of the cause, from one party to the other. The party agreeing to indemnify the other party is agreeing to accept the costs of defending any lawsuits, as well as agreeing to pay any resulting settlements, fees, fines, and so on as a result of the lawsuit.[20] Accordingly, indemnification clauses present significant risk. They are common in contracts. Many, if not most, government agencies are legally prohibited from agreeing to indemnification clauses.

Indemnification clauses can be either one-way or mutual. Be sure to read your contract drafts carefully to determine whether the indemnification provision applies to both parties or only to one party.

Please note that an indemnification clause does not need to contain the word "indemnity" (or any derivative of that word) to function as an indemnification clause. The word "indemnify," or any derivative of that word, is not a "magic word." So, be sure to review contracts carefully for language that imposes an indemnification obligation without using the word "indemnify" or similar language. For example, a clause might require your organization to accept "all liability, regardless of cause, and regardless of fault."

Model language[21] ("Acme" is a placeholder for your organization):
12. **Indemnification.** (a) With respect to any Proceeding brought by someone other than the Vendor or someone other than one or more Acme Indemnitees against one or more Acme Indemnitees and that arises out of this agreement or Acme's purchase or use of Units (each, a "**Nonparty Claim**"), the Vendor shall

indemnify those Acme Indemnitees against all Indemnifiable Losses arising out of that Proceeding, except to the extent that Acme negligently or intentionally caused those Indemnifiable Losses.

(b) To be entitled to indemnification under Section 12(a), an Acme Indemnitee subject to any Nonparty Claim must promptly (and in any event no later than 10 days after the Acme Indemnitee first knew of that Nonparty Claim) notify the Vendor of that Nonparty Claim and deliver to the Vendor a copy of all legal pleadings with respect to the Nonparty Claim. If the Acme Indemnitee fails to timely notify the Vendor of a Nonparty Claim, the Vendor will be relieved of its indemnification obligations with respect to that Nonparty Claim to the extent that the Vendor was prejudiced by that failure and the Vendor will not be required to reimburse the Acme Indemnitee for any Litigation Expenses the Acme Indemnitee incurred during the period in which the Acme Indemnitee failed to notify the Vendor.

(c) To assume the defense of a Nonparty Claim, the Vendor must notify the Acme Indemnitee that it is doing so. Promptly thereafter, the Vendor shall retain to represent it in the Nonparty Claim independent legal counsel that is reasonably acceptable to the Acme Indemnitee.

(d) An Acme Indemnitee is entitled to participate in the defense of a Nonparty Claim. An Acme Indemnitee may defend a Nonparty Claim with counsel of its own choosing and without the Vendor participating if (1) the Vendor notifies the Acme Indemnitee that it does not wish to defend the Nonparty Claim, (2) by midnight at the end of the tenth day[22] after the Acme Indemnitee notifies the Vendor of the Nonparty Claim the Vendor fails to notify the Acme Indemnitee that it wishes to defend the Nonparty Claim, or (3) representation of the Vendor and the Acme Indemnitee by the same counsel would, in the opinion of that counsel, constitute a conflict of interest.

(e) The Vendor shall pay any Litigation Expenses that an Acme Indemnitee incurs in connection with defense of the Nonparty Claim before the Vendor assumes the defense of that Nonparty Claim, except with respect to any period during which the Acme Indemnitee fails to timely notify the Vendor of that Nonparty Claim. The Vendor will not be liable for any Litigation Expenses that a Acme Indemnitee incurs in connection with defense of a Nonparty Claim after the Vendor assumes the defense of that Nonparty Claim, other than Litigation Expenses that the Acme Indemnitee incurs in employing counsel in accordance with Section 12(d), which Litigation Expenses the Vendor shall pay promptly as they are incurred.

(f) After the Vendor assumes the defense of a Nonparty Claim, the Vendor may contest, pay, or settle the Nonparty Claim without the consent of the Acme Indemnitee only if that settlement (1) does not entail any admission on the part of the Acme Indemnitee that it violated any law or infringed the rights of any Person, (2) has no effect on any other claim against the Acme Indemnitee, (3) provides as the claimant's sole relief monetary damages that are paid in full by the Vendor, and (4) requires that the claimant release the Acme Indemnitee from all liability alleged in the Nonparty Claim.

(g) In this agreement, the following definitions apply:

"**Acme Indemnitee**" means Acme; any Affiliate of Acme; each Representative of any of the foregoing; and each of the heirs, executors, successors, and assignees of any of the foregoing.

"**Indemnifiable Losses**" means the aggregate of Losses and Litigation Expenses.

"**Litigation Expense**" means any [reasonable] out-of-pocket expense incurred in defending a Proceeding or in any related investigation or negotiation, including court filing fees, court costs, arbitration fees, witness fees, and attorneys' and other professionals' fees and disbursements.

"**Loss**" means any amount awarded in, or paid in settlement of, any Proceeding, including any interest but excluding any Litigation Expenses.

"**Proceeding**" means any judicial; administrative; or arbitration action, suit, claim, investigation, or proceeding.

"**Representative**" means, with respect to an entity, any of that entity's directors, officers, employees, agents, consultants, advisors, and other representatives.

Insurance

When you encounter a clause requiring your organization to buy insurance, or if you are considering requiring the other party to maintain insurance, be sure to consult with your risk management office or the other appropriate office within your organization.

If a contract requires your organization to have insurance, be sure to determine whether your organization, in fact, maintains the required insurance before you agree to the clause. More importantly, ensure that your organization intends to maintain the required insurance for the duration of the contract.

When your organization requires suppliers to maintain insurance, determine who in your organization will verify the coverage by receiving the supplier's insurance certificate. When will your organization require the supplier to provide you with the certificate? The best practice would be to require the supplier to provide your organization with their insurance certificate before your organization signs the contract.

Insurance certificates typically expire annually. Consider how your organization will track insurance certificates' validity period, who will monitor expirations, and who will follow up with suppliers to obtain any renewal certificates.

In our model language here, we assume that the insurance language is placed in a "schedule." Moreover, we have assumed that the supplier will provide proof of insurance before the supplier signs the contract. The model language accounts for the following items:

- Naming your organization as an additional insured entity
- Requiring the supplier's insurance to be primary and noncontributory

- Defines the minimal standards for the supplier's insurance to be acceptable to your organization
- Requires the supplier to verify their insurance coverage
- Accounts for whether the supplier's subcontractors carry adequate insurance or that the supplier's subcontractors are covered by the supplier's policy
- Lists the types of insurance that your organization requires the supplier to maintain

Model language:

Schedule 1

Supplier must comply with the following requirements:

1. **Additional Insurance Requirements:** The policies must include, or be endorsed to include, the following provisions:
   a. On insurance policies where [name of your organization] is named as an additional insured. [Name of your organization] must be an additional insured to the full limits of liability purchased by Supplier, even if those limits of liability are in excess of those required by this contract.
   b. Supplier's insurance coverage must be primary insurance and noncontributory with respect to all other available sources.
2. **Effective Period; Notice of Cancellation:** Supplier will make reasonable efforts to ensure that all insurance coverage required below remains in effect for the duration of this agreement. Supplier must notify [name of your organization] within 30 days of any of the following events: Supplier cancels one or more policies required by this agreement, Supplier modifies the limits of coverage for any policy required by this agreement, or the insurance provider cancels any policy or modifies any policy required by this agreement. Supplier will notify [name of your organization] by contacting:

   [notice address for your organization's risk management office]

3. **Acceptability of Insurers:** Supplier must provide insurance through an insurer licensed to do business in the state of [state where your organization is located] and with an A.M. Best rating of not less than A-VII.[23]
4. **Verification of Coverage:** Supplier must provide [name of your organization] with certificates of insurance (ACORD form or equivalent) documenting each policy required by this agreement. The certificates for each insurance policy must be signed by a person authorized by that insurer to bind coverage on its behalf.
5. **Subcontractors:** Supplier's certificate(s) must include all subcontractors as additional insureds under Supplier's policies, or Supplier must furnish [name of your organization] separate certificates and endorsements for each subcontractor. All coverages for subcontractors must be subject to the minimum requirements identified in this schedule.

6. **Required Coverage**: During the term of this agreement, Supplier must maintain the following insurance types and limits (or higher limits):

[here, insert the type of insurance with the
minimum coverage required]

[example:]

[Workers' Compensation (WC):

Employers' Liability Each Accident	$100,000
Employers' Liability Disease—each employee	$100,000
Employers' Liability Disease—policy limit	$500,000

Commercial General Liability (CGL):

Each Occurrence Limit	$1,000,000
Damage to Rented Premises—Ea. Occ.	$300,000
Medical Expense—any one person	$10,000
Personal and Advertising Injury Limit	$1,000,000
General Aggregate Limit	$2,000,000
Products/Completed Ops. Aggregate Limit	$2,000,000

Automobile Liability:

Combined Single Limit	$1,000,000]

Limitation of Action

Most crimes, and most civil causes of action, have a "shelf life," and after the "expiration date," no one may bring legal action over the issue. Most people call the laws that create the "shelf life" by the name "statute of limitations," but the legal term is "limitation of action." Note that some states have enacted laws such that limitations of actions on civil cases do not apply to the government.

A common statutory limitation of action for contract claims is six years. Because companies want to minimize their exposure to litigation, sometimes companies will include a contractual limitation of action—that is, a clause in their contracts that limits the time during which either party may bring a claim against the other that arises out of the contract.

In certain circumstances, most courts view contractual limitations of action clauses as enforceable.[24] In most circumstances, limiting your right to bring a contract claim might not be problematic. In some circumstances, however, it might be problematic to limit your ability to file a lawsuit to less than the default time set by statute.

Carefully consider the consequences of agreeing to limit your ability to file a lawsuit and negotiate with the other party accordingly.

Example:
Neither party may bring an action on this agreement more than 12 months after it accrues.

Options:
- Agree to the clause.

- Delete the clause entirely. If your organization is a government agency, this approach might be the only one you can take for contractual limitations of action. If your organization is not a government agency, you might find it difficult to find sufficient reasoning to delete the language entirely.

- Modify the language by adding "to the extent allowed by _____ [specific state, such as New York] law . . .", or perhaps "to the extent allowed by applicable law," in front of the limitation of action clause. This approach is common with some governmental organizations, but please be sure to consult with your attorney before using this approach. If your organization already uses this approach, be sure to consult with your attorney to determine whether this is an approach that your organization needs to continue.

Liquidated Damages

Generally speaking, "penalties" are unenforceable in contracts. Notably, "prepayment penalties" are generally allowable in loan agreements, but courts generally refuse to enforce other types of contract payments that serve as penalties.[25] Accordingly, your organization must avoid calling a fee or payment a "penalty." Further, carefully consider cancellation fees and similar matters before including them in a contract. If you set such fees too high, it is possible that a court could find that the fees are an unenforceable penalty.[26] A liquidated damage clause occurs where the parties agree to a specific amount of money that one party would owe the other in the event of breach.[27] Liquidated damage clauses are typically used when the parties believe that it would be impractical to calculate damages.[28]

Model language[29] *("Acme" and "Widgetco" are placeholders; in the wording that follows, Acme will pay Widgetco liquidated damages if Acme breaches):*
Acme acknowledges that the actual damages likely to result from breach of this Section X are difficult to estimate on the date of this agreement and would be difficult for Widgetco to prove. The parties intend that Acme's payment of the Liquidated Damages Amount would serve to compensate Widgetco for any breach by Acme of its obligations under this Section X, and they do not intend for it to serve as punishment for any such breach by Acme.

Modification Waiver (or Amendment)

This is sometimes called the "no oral modification" or "no verbal modification" clause. Generally, the best practice is to avoid situations where either party claims that the contract was modified by verbal discussions. To help ensure that the parties express their intent that the parties may only modify the agreement by written amendment,[30] the best practice is to use a no oral modification clause.

Model language:
No amendment of this agreement will be effective unless it is in writing and signed by the parties. No waiver of satisfaction of a condition or failure to comply with an obligation under this agreement will be effective unless it is in writing and signed by the party granting the waiver, and no such waiver will constitute a waiver of satisfaction of any other condition or failure to comply with any other obligation.

If your organization is large, and especially if it is large and decentralized, consider whether it would be advantageous for your organization to communicate to its suppliers who at your organization has signature authority. The advantage to communicating who has signature authority at your organization is that it will help your suppliers know when someone has signed without authority. If you work for a centralized organization, it might sound unusual (or perhaps even unbelievable) that an organization would struggle with people without signature authority signing contracts. Large, decentralized organizations (especially universities) struggle with unauthorized signatures often (conceivably on a daily basis).

Including the additional language at the end of the clause here ("To be valid, any document signed by Customer must be signed by an official of Licensee who has signature authority; a website listing of Licensee's officials with signature authority is located here: _____.") only helps so much because it only reaches vendors who see your contracts. End users and other vendors who work with your organization outside of contracts will never see that language.

Model language for large, decentralized organizations:
No amendment of this agreement will be effective unless it is in writing and signed by the parties. No waiver of satisfaction of a condition or failure to comply with an obligation under this agreement will be effective unless it is in writing and signed by the party granting the waiver, and no such waiver will constitute a waiver of satisfaction of any other condition or failure to comply with any other obligation. To be valid, any document signed by Customer must be signed by an official of Licensee who has signature authority; a website listing of Licensee's officials with signature authority is located here: _____.

Multiple Languages

The optimal practice is to ensure that the parties negotiate one contract, in one language. Many government agencies and other nonprofit organizations enter into contracts with organizations based in countries other than the United States. For purposes of this book, we will consider organizations outside of the United States as "foreign corporations." Often, those foreign corporations use a primary language other than English. Regardless of location, however, many foreign corporations choose to draft contracts in English. After all, English is virtually the international business language.[31]

When contracting with foreign corporations, your organization might encounter one of three scenarios:

1. The foreign corporation wants your organization to sign a contract only in a foreign language.
2. The foreign corporation wants your organization to sign two contracts, which apply to one transaction, but with one contract in a foreign language and one contract in English.
3. The foreign corporation wants your organization to sign one contract, where the contract contains two versions of each clause: one in a foreign language and one in English.

Model language:
The parties agree that this agreement has been drafted and signed in English and _____[foreign language] and that the parties intend for all versions of this agreement to contain identical terms and conditions, regardless of the language used. Notwithstanding any other provision of this agreement which may appear to be to the contrary, in the event that any version of this agreement does not contain all of the terms and conditions included in the English version, or in the event that any version contains any terms and conditions that either conflict with, are contrary to, or are in addition to the terms and conditions contained in the English version, the English version will prevail over such other versions and be controlling and legally binding on the parties.

Fall-back model language:
The parties agree that, in the event of a conflict between the documents, the English-language translation of the agreement will govern and control.

Nonsolicitation

A nonsolicitation clause (which might be called a "covenant not to hire") attempts to prevent one party (or all parties) from hiring the other party's employees for a certain period. These clauses are common with consulting agreements and outsourced service agreements, such as information technology, concessions/pouring rights, food service, or bookstore operations.

The primary challenge with this type of clause is that many large organizations do not track nonsolicitation clauses. This is due to the inherent disconnect between the organization's human resources department (primarily involved in internal issues and recruiting) and the organization's contract review function. So, while the organization's contract review officials might approve of the nonsolicitation clause, the organization's human resource function likely will not even know about the clause (and, even if they do, there would be challenges involved in tracking the clause due to the fact that the supplier's staff will change over time). If your organization is willing to agree to this type of clause, be sure to coordinate with your organization's human resources office first to understand the human resources office's general thoughts on this type of clause. Further, consider including the human resources office as part of the review process whenever your organization encounters this type of clause.

The next challenge with this type of clause is that the typical language in a nonsolicitation clause prohibits your organization from hiring anyone who works for the supplier. If the supplier has more than a handful of employees, it will likely be impossible for your organization to know who works for the supplier.

Another issue with this type of clause is that the typical language places long-term prohibitions on your organization. For example, the clause will prohibit your organization from hiring any of the supplier's employees during the term of the agreement between your organization and the supplier and for 6 to 18 months after the agreement expires or is terminated.

Although not very common, you might encounter an issue where the supplier's language prohibits your organization from hiring any of its employees and prohibits your organization from using any of the supplier's contractors and any of the supplier's contractor's subcontractors. This restriction presents the same issues as noted earlier, just with a much broader scope.

The "bottom line" on nonsolicitation clauses is that they are easy to breach. Not only is the typical human resources office separated from the contract review function but the scope of the typical nonsolicitation clause applies to too many of supplier's employees for too long of a time.

Options:
- Delete the clause entirely.

  - If your organization's human resources office does not track this sort of clause, tell the supplier that fact. There is nothing wrong with being honest about this specific item.

  - Your organization could argue that people ought to have freedom of choice when it comes to work and that the organization does not support the notion of prohibiting anyone from applying for its open positions.

- If you cannot get the supplier to agree to delete the clause, focus on limiting the duration and scope (breadth) of the clause.

   o Restrict the clause such that it only applies when your organization
     actively solicits/recruits one of the supplier's staff members. In other
     words, your organization does not breach the agreement if one of the
     supplier's staff members applies for an open position within your organ-
     ization as long as your organization did not recruit that person.

   o Restrict the clause to named individuals. Further, require the supplier to
     provide you with the then-current version of all individuals covered by the
     clause. Specify that your organization is not liable for hiring someone if
     their name is not on the list at the time your organization hires the person.
     Be sure to define what point in time the "hiring" takes place, such as when
     your organization makes an offer.

Notice

The purpose of a notice clause is to define how the parties will communicate with each other regarding formal communications under the contract.
For example, if a party wanted to terminate a contract, the party would need
to deliver notice to the other by following the notice clause.

Sample clause:

(a) For a notice or other communication under this agreement to be valid, it
must be in writing and delivered (1) by hand; (2) by a national transportation company, with all fees prepaid; or (3) by registered or certified mail,
return receipt requested and postage prepaid.

(b) Subject to Section 10(d), a valid notice or other communication under
this agreement will be effective when received by the party to which it is
addressed. It will be deemed to have been received as follows:

   (1) if it is delivered by hand; delivered by a national transportation com-
     pany, with all fees prepaid; or delivered by registered or certified mail,
     return receipt requested and postage prepaid, upon receipt as indicated
     by the date on the signed receipt; and

   (2) if the party to which it is addressed rejects or otherwise refuses to
     accept it, or if it cannot be delivered because of a change in address
     for which no notice was given, then upon that rejection, refusal, or
     inability to deliver.

(c) For a notice or other communication to a party under this agreement to
be valid, it must be addressed using the information specified below for that
party or any other information specified by that party in a notice in accordance with this Section 10.

   To Licensee:

           The University of _____

           Address line

           Address line

City, State ZIP Code

Attention:

Email address

To Licensor:

Licensor's name

Address line

Address line

City, State ZIP Code

Attention:

Email address

(d) If a notice or other communication addressed to a party is received after 5:00 p.m. on a business day at the location specified in the address for that party or on a day that is not a business day, then the notice will be deemed received at 9:00 a.m. on the next business day.

Online Terms

Many companies have click-through, shrink-wrap, or other online terms and conditions. Many times, these types of agreements are referred to as "EULAs," or "end-user license agreements."

Generally speaking, there are two broad types of electronic terms and conditions:

1. *Browse-wrap (also known as browserwrap or browse-wrap license):* In a browse-wrap agreement, the terms and conditions of use for a website or other downloadable product are posted on the website, typically as a hyperlink at the bottom of the screen. Unlike a clickwrap agreement, where the user must manifestly assent to the terms and conditions by clicking on an "I agree" box, a browse-wrap agreement does not require this type of express manifestation of assent. Rather, a website user purportedly gives his or her assent by simply using the product—such as by entering the website or downloading software.

2. *Clickwrap (also known as click-wrap, click-through, or click-to-accept):* Users are prompted to actively indicate their acceptance of terms and conditions (for example, by checking a box, clicking "I agree," etc.).

Click-wrap agreements are generally considered legally binding in the United States. Whether browse-wrap agreements are enforceable is controversial, but let's assume for our purposes that they are legally binding. Even though click-through, shrink-wrap, or other online terms and conditions are not signed like a traditional contract, they are legally binding.

Note that these types of agreements have lots of different names, including but not limited to the following:

- Browse-wrap
- Click-to-accept
- Click-wrap
- Terms of service
- Terms of use
- Wrap agreements

These types of agreements are problematic because the online or shrink-wrap terms and conditions could contradict any agreement between your organization and a supplier. Another problematic issue is that, almost always, the person allegedly agreeing on behalf of an organization is a departmental staff member and not someone who has signature authority. Also, terms and conditions that are electronic can be changed at any time (i.e., the other party has a unilateral right to modify the terms and conditions).

There are three general types of terms and conditions:

- *Click-through, clickwrap, click-wrap, or click-to-accept:* The end user must signify their acceptance of the license terms in some manner, usually by clicking "I agree."
- *Shrink-wrap:* The terms and conditions are included with, and often affixed to, the item that the user is using, such as a seal over a product that says: "By using this product, you agree to the terms and conditions listed on Vendor's website, located at . . .".
- *Browserwrap, browsewrap, browse-wrap, TOS, terms of service, terms of use:* Most websites have only a set of terms and conditions located on the site, and use of the website constitutes agreement to the terms and conditions. Often, the link will be labeled "Legal," "Legal Notice," or "Terms of Use."

Practically every supplier has a website, and most websites contain electronic terms and conditions in some format. The following language should be inserted into every contract where your organization is acquiring a good or service from a company.

Option 1 (best case): The best case is when the supplier agrees that the click-through agreement does not apply to your organization. If the supplier will agree to this, then the following language must be used.

Model language:
This agreement constitutes the entire understanding between the parties with respect to the subject matter of this agreement and supersedes all other

agreements, whether written or oral, between the parties. In the event that Supplier's goods or services contain electronic terms and conditions, Supplier states that such terms and conditions do not apply to [name of your organization].

Option 2: However, in many cases, the supplier will not agree to remove the click-through language. In such case, try to get the supplier to agree that the click-through language does not apply to the organization but only to the end users as individuals.

Model language:
The parties agree that the click-through and other online terms and conditions apply to end users in their individual capacity (but do not apply to the organization).

Option 3: If the supplier objects to both options 1 and 2, the next best option would be to revise the click-through language such that it is acceptable to the organization.

Option 4: If the supplier objects to options 1 to 3, then the last option would be to revise specific provisions of the click-through agreement and state that those key provisions can only be modified in a written amendment that is signed by authorized officials of both parties. Key provisions would be governing law, the organization's liability, and so on. The following is an example of an addendum that would cover the most important provisions.

Prevailing Terms Addendum

This prevailing terms agreement is dated _____, 20___, and is between [your organization's legal name], [your organization's legal structure] [in this example, the model organization is a university] ("University"), and _____, a/an _____ ("Supplier").

Background:

    A. The University utilizes Supplier's website to conduct business with Supplier.

    B. Supplier's website contains terms and conditions ("terms of use").

    C. The University, as an instrumentality of the State of Tennessee, cannot agree to certain terms and conditions.

(continued)

Agreement:

The parties agree as follows:

1. **Precedence**: The parties intend for the terms of this agreement to prevail over any conflicting terms in Supplier's terms of use. Supplier states that any conflicting terms in Supplier's terms of use are deleted.
2. **University's Indemnification of Supplier**: The University will not indemnify, defend, or hold harmless Supplier. Supplier states that there are no circumstances under which University would indemnify, defend, or hold harmless Supplier.
3. **Governing Law**: The laws of the state of Tennessee, without giving effect to its principles of conflicts of law, govern this agreement. The United Nations Convention on Contracts for the International Sale of Goods does not apply to transactions between the University and Supplier.
4. **Venue**: In the event that Supplier files a lawsuit against University, Supplier will only file a lawsuit in the Tennessee Claims Commission.
5. **Automatic Renewal**: Supplier acknowledges that the University cannot agree to a term that automatically renews if the automatic renewal would require the University to incur any costs.
6. **Fees and Costs**: The University will not pay Supplier's attorneys' fees, court costs, costs of collection, or costs of an audit.
7. **Third-Party Beneficiaries**: No person or entity, other than the University and Supplier and their successors and permitted assigns has any rights, remedies, claims, benefits, or powers under this agreement, and this agreement will not be construed or interpreted to confer any rights, remedies, claims, benefits, or powers upon any third party. There are no third-party beneficiaries of this agreement.
8. **Insurance**: Except for shipping/transit insurance, the University will not buy insurance or name the Supplier as an additional insured.
9. **Confidentiality**: The University's obligation to keep information confidential will not apply if disclosure is required by state or federal law or regulations, including without limitation, the Tennessee Public Records Act, Tenn. Code Ann. § 10-7-503. The existence of any agreement between Supplier and University is not confidential.

10. **Sovereign Immunity**: Any provisions stating that the University waives sovereign immunity do not apply to the University.

11. **Exclusivity**: Any agreement between University and Supplier is not exclusive.

12. **Nonsolicitation**: Any clause prohibiting the University from hiring Supplier's employees, officers, contractors, or suppliers does not apply to the University.

13. **Counterparts**: If the parties sign this agreement in several counterparts, each will be deemed an original, but all counterparts together will constitute one instrument.

14. **Modification; Waiver; Authorized Signature**: No amendment of this agreement will be effective unless it is in writing and signed by authorized officials of the parties. No waiver of satisfaction of a condition or failure to comply with an obligation under this agreement will be effective unless it is in writing and signed by the party granting the waiver, and no such waiver will constitute a waiver of satisfaction of any other condition or failure to comply with any other obligation. To be valid, any document signed by the University in accordance with this section must be signed by an official listed on this website: [insert your organization's website listing authorized signatories here].

15. **Entire Agreement**: This agreement constitutes the entire understanding between the parties with respect to the subject matter of this agreement and supersedes all other agreements, whether written or oral, between the parties.

The parties are signing this agreement on the date stated in the introductory clause:

[Your organization]	Supplier
Signature:_____	Signature:_____
Name:_____	Name:_____
Title:_____	Title:_____

Primary Vendor

The concept of a primary vendor might arise in one of two contexts. First, a vendor might mistakenly use the word "primary" in an attempt to express an exclusivity obligation.[32] For example, a vendor (Acme Travel Solutions) who provided travel management services described itself as the primary vendor for the University of Cats regarding sports team travel. The University of Cats failed to question, much less strike, the use of the word "primary" in the contract. During the last year of the contract, the University of Cats used Pinnacle Travel Solutions for most, but not all, of its team travel. Acme Travel Solutions complained to the University of Cats that its contract with the university was exclusive due to the use of the word "primary." On its face, the vendor's argument was clearly wrong because the dictionary definition of primary means "first"; it does not mean "sole" or "only" (for example, many people have a primary care physician, and that physician is never intended to be a patient's only doctor; skydivers have a primary parachute, which is obviously not intended to be the sole parachute). Nevertheless, the vendor was very upset when their president found out that the university utilized Pinnacle Travel Solutions. Acme threatened to sue but never did. While the university would have easily won a lawsuit over whether the word "primary" meant "exclusive," the university's failure to strike the word "primary" resulted in a significant business relationship issue between the university and the vendor.

Second, some government (particularly higher education) procurement departments engage in a practice of naming one vendor preferred and another vendor (or other vendors) secondary. The thought behind this practice is that the primary vendor is favored, and if the primary vendor is unable or unwilling to perform the work, the organization would be able to utilize the secondary vendor(s). Although this concept might sound worthwhile in theory, in reality, it can be very difficult to enforce. Creating a primary and secondary vendor setup can create audit problems for the university, as well as business relationship problems. The former would arise if an internal audit found that the university failed to honor the primary vs. secondary designation, and the latter would arise if the primary vendor found out that the university utilized the secondary vendor without first contacting the primary vendor.

Requirements

A requirements clause is a clause where the parties agree that the customer will buy all of its needed quantity of a particular item, or particular items, exclusively from the seller. The purpose of the clause is to allow the seller to plan their output and income based on anticipated volume, and, in exchange, the buyer can anticipate a better price than if buying on the open market. Requirements clauses are risky for any organization that has any decentralized purchasing privileges.

If your organization allows end users the ability to make small purchases (sometimes called "micro purchases") without going through a central purchasing office for approval, then your organization would be well served to prohibit requirements obligations in contracts. Although there can be some efficiency benefits by allowing end users the power to make small purchases without seeking formal approval from central purchasing, the downside to allowing this is that the organization loses the ability to control its purchasing.

A requirements clause is a type of exclusivity obligation. In the next section, we will consider exclusivity obligations, generally, and recommended best practices for how to manage the exclusivity obligations, specifically.

Severability

The purpose of a severability clause is for the parties to express their intent that a court enforce the contract to the extent possible when a court finds that one or more of a contract's clauses are unenforceable.[33] In other words, severability clauses help express to a court that the parties intended to draft a fully enforceable contract and that the parties want a court to enforce the legally enforceable parts of the contract if a court finds that some of the contract is not enforceable.

Model language:
Section #:
  a. That if any provision of this agreement is held to be unenforceable, then that provision will be modified to the minimum extent necessary to make it enforceable, unless that modification is not permitted by law, in which case that provision will be disregarded;

  b. That if an unenforceable provision is modified or disregarded in accordance with this Severability section, then the rest of the agreement will remain in effect as written; and

  c. That any unenforceable provision will remain as written in any circumstances other than those in which the provision is held to be unenforceable.

Supplier Conduct

When suppliers will be on your organization's property, consider what type of interactions they might have with your organization's employees, customers (including library patrons and students), and visitors. Delivery and maintenance staff might have substantial interaction with your organization's employees, customers, and visitors.

One of the co-authors handled a situation where a furniture company outsourced delivery to a subcontractor and at least one of the subcontractor's staff members made inappropriate remarks to some people who worked for a university. That incident led the co-authors to account for this type of scenario in their contracts.

When a supplier will interact with your organization's employees, customers, and visitors, consider asking the supplier to describe the supplier's rules for sexual harassment, what type of training the supplier provides, and whether the supplier either educates its subcontractors or requires subcontractors to educate their staff.

Consider also whether you want to require the supplier to conduct background checks for its employees, subcontractors, and so on. If so, consider issues such as timing (does the supplier need to have the background checks completed before the supplier starts work?) and issues such as whether the supplier needs to run background checks more than once on the same employees (for example, annually).

Model language:
Background Checks:
   a. *General obligation*: Supplier will not knowingly assign any individual to provide services to [organization] if the individual has a history of criminal conduct. For proposes of this agreement, "criminal conduct" means charges filed by any government agency, excluding nonmoving violations and speeding violations.

   b. [Add specific language regarding statutes or registries in your state. Here is an example of a Tennessee-specific clause:] Tennessee Abuse Registry; Tennessee Sex Offender: Supplier must inform the University's Office of Procurement Services immediately if any of Supplier's employees or subcontractors are listed in:

      i. The Tennessee Abuse Registry

      ii. The Tennessee Sex Offender Registry

   c. *Prompt background checks*: If the [organization] requests, Supplier must perform a comprehensive criminal background check on any Supplier employee or subcontractor.

Premises Rules: When Supplier is physically present on University property, Supplier shall make reasonable efforts to cause its employees and permitted subcontractors to become aware of, and in full compliance with, [organization's] rules, practices, and policies (collectively referred to as "rules"). For example, Supplier shall ensure that it complies with the [organization's] applicable rules regarding safety, smoking, noise, access restrictions, parking, security, and consideration for minors (students and visitors under age 18).

Conduct: Supplier will make reasonable efforts to ensure that Supplier's employees and subcontractors will conduct themselves in a professional manner while on [organization's] property and while interacting with [organization's] employees, students, or visitors. Supplier must report within 24 hours to the [organization's] [list specific office] any complaints about Supplier's employees or subcontractors engaging in the following behavior: sexually suggestive or harassing behavior; unwanted physical touching; unwanted photographs; alcohol use; illegal drug use; or physical manifestations of alcohol or drug use (e.g., Supplier's employee emits smells that indicate that the individual consumed alcohol recently).

Third-Party Beneficiary

A third-party beneficiary is an individual or organization that is not a party to the contract but has the right to enforce a promise in the contract.[34] Sometimes, a supplier's contract will provide that one or more third-party companies are third-party beneficiaries to a contract. Naming third-party beneficiaries increases the number of entities that can sue your organization to enforce the contract.

If your organization is a government agency, be sure to determine whether your state's law allows third-party beneficiaries to bring claims. If it does not, consider either 1) adding language to the contract stating that there are no third-party beneficiaries to the contract or 2) adding the would-be third-party beneficiary as a party to the contract.

Termination/Cancellation

In your organization's contract, be sure to specify when either party may cancel each contract. The best practice is to avoid using language that refers to "cancellation for convenience." That phrase is unclear and, more to the point, does not express the concept that your organization may cancel at any time for any reason as clearly as possible.

Model language:
Unrestricted Termination. Acme may terminate this agreement for any reason by giving the Vendor at least 30 days' prior notice.[35]

Venue (or Jurisdiction or Forum Selection)

Because each state's laws vary, most organizations like to limit their risk by requiring that contract disputes take place in the organization's favored venue. An organization might favor one venue over the other because the venue has well-developed business law (for example, Delaware courts) or because the venue is within a close geographic proximity to the organization. Venue-selection clauses are generally enforceable.[36]

When you evaluate a venue-selection clause, determine whether the clause is mandatory/exclusive (that is, restricts the parties' ability to file suit to one specific venue) or permissive (that is, the parties consent to jurisdiction in the stated venue or venues, but the plaintiff may file in any venue that has jurisdiction over the defendant).[37]

CONCLUSION

Maintaining a solid understanding of common types of contract clauses will empower you to approach contracts with more confidence and allow you to be more efficient when reviewing contracts. In the next chapter, we consider special clauses that appear often in certain types of transactions.

NOTES

1. Stark, Tina L., *Drafting Contracts: How and Why Lawyers Do What They Do*, New York: Wolters Kluwer Law & Business (2nd ed.), p. 154.
2. Stark, *Drafting Contracts*, p. 154.
3. Stark, *Drafting Contracts*, p. 154.
4. Adams, Ken, "Rethinking the 'No Assignment' Provision," http://www.adamsdrafting.com/rethinking-the-no-assignment-provision (cited March 4, 2019).
5. Adams, Ken, "Rethinking the 'No Assignment' Provision."
6. Rogers, Brian, "Attorney Fees in Contracts," https://thecontractsguy.net/2018/01/28/attorney-fees-contracts (cited March 4, 2019).
7. Oswald Companies, "Prevailing Opinions on Prevailing Party Contract Clauses," https://www.oswaldcompanies.com/wp-content/uploads/2014/09/Prevailing-Opinions-on-Prevailing-Party-Contract-Clauses-Read-Only.pdf (cited March 4, 2019).
8. Price Waterhouse Coopers, "Counterparts Boilerplate Clause," https://www.pwc.com.au/legal/assets/investing-in-infrastructure/iif-26-counterparts-boiler plate-clause-feb16-2.pdf (cited March 4, 2019).
9. The Judicial Branch of California, "ADR Types & Benefits," http://www.courts.ca.gov/3074.htm (cited March 4, 2019).
10. Stark, Tina, *Negotiating and Drafting Contract Boilerplate*, New York: ALM Publishing, 2003, p. 561.
11. Stark, *Negotiating and Drafting Contract Boilerplate*, pp. 560–566.
12. Stark, *Negotiating and Drafting Contract Boilerplate*, pp. 561–562.
13. Stark, *Negotiating and Drafting Contract Boilerplate*, p. 327.
14. Stark, *Negotiating and Drafting Contract Boilerplate*, p. 328.
15. Stark, *Negotiating and Drafting Contract Boilerplate*, p. 328.
16. Adams, Ken, "Revisiting My 'Force Majeure' Language (with Yet More Changes)," https://www.adamsdrafting.com/revisiting-my-force-majeure-lan guage (cited March 4, 2019).
17. Forbes, "What Exactly Is Indemnification, and How Does It Affect a Free-lance Contributor," https://www.forbes.com/sites/artneill/2018/11/14/what-exactly-is-indemnification-and-how-does-it-affect-a-freelance-contributor/#95f7efe6f102 (cited March 4, 2019).
18. Adams, Jen, "'Hold Harmless' and 'Indemnity,'" https://www.adamsdrafting.com/hold-harmless-and-indemnify (cited March 4, 2019).
19. Harroch, Richard, *Business Contracts Kit for Dummies*, New York: Wiley Publishing, 2000, p. 25.
20. Harroch, Richard, *Business Contracts Kit for Dummies*, p. 25.

21. Adams, Ken, "My Indemnification Language," https://www.adamsdrafting
    .com/my-indemnification-language (cited March 4, 2019).

22. See MSCD, p. 249, Section 10.72. Within a contract, the best practice might
    be to state that any reference to days means "business days." If you do that in
    one paragraph, you will not have to refer to "business days" every time you
    refer to "days."

23. A.M. Best is an insurance rating organization. "A" is the highest rating avail-
    able. The "VII" is a shorthand reference to the financial stability of the insur-
    ance company. See https://www.thebalance.com/what-is-an-a-rated-insurance
    -company-and-why-does-it-matter-4065596; see also http://www.cblinsurance
    .com/UserFiles/CBLInsurance/File/Understanding%20AM%20Best%20
    Ratings.pdf

24. Rogers, Brian, "Contractual Limitations: Why Are You Suing Me When Our
    Contract Says You Can't," https://thecontractsguy.net/2012/11/30/contractual
    -limitations-why-are-you-suing-me-when-our-contract-says-you-cant (cited
    March 4, 2019).

25. Stark, *Negotiating and Drafting Contract Boilerplate*, p. 228.

26. Stark, *Negotiating and Drafting Contract Boilerplate*, pp. 227–228.

27. Stark, *Negotiating and Drafting Contract Boilerplate*, p. 225.

28. Stark, *Negotiating and Drafting Contract Boilerplate*, p. 225.

29. Adams, Ken, "'As Liquidated Damages and Not as a Penalty,'" https://
    www.adamsdrafting.com/as-liquidated-damages-and-not-as-a-penalty (cited
    March 4, 2019).

30. Stark, *Negotiating and Drafting Contract Boilerplate*, p. 527.

31. Adams, *A Manual of Style for Contract Drafting*, p. xxxiv.

32. This is based on a real example.

33. Stark, *Negotiating and Drafting Contract Boilerplate*, p. 541.

34. Burnham, Scott J., *Contract Law for Dummies*. Hoboken: John Wiley &
    Sons, 2012, p. 306.

35. Adams, Ken, "Termination for Convenience," http://www.adamsdrafting
    .com/termination-for-convenience (cited March 4, 2019).

36. Stark, *Negotiating and Drafting Contract Boilerplate*, p. 131.

37. Stark, *Negotiating and Drafting Contract Boilerplate*, 128–129; 137–140.

Managing Contracts*

INTRODUCTION

In this chapter, we will discuss several topics that are common in specific types of transactions, for example, hotel contracts. When combined with the previous chapter, the information in this chapter will provide readers with well-rounded background material to face almost any type of transaction that libraries will encounter.

SPECIFIC TRANSACTIONS AND SPECIAL TOPICS

Intellectual Property

Patent Law. Patent law protects inventions, and patent holders have the exclusive right to make, use, sell, and import their invention and the right to prevent others from doing so.

Copyright Law. Copyright, a form of intellectual property law, protects original works of authorship, including literary, dramatic, musical, and artistic works, such as poetry, novels, movies, songs, computer software, and architecture. Copyright does not protect facts, ideas, systems, or methods of operation, although it may protect the way these things are expressed. The copyright owner does have certain exclusive rights in the copyrighted work and the right to allow others to do any of the following:

---

*Parts of this chapter are based on Halaychik, Corey S. and Blake Reagan, "Basics of Licensing Law," in *Licensing Electronic Resources in Academic Libraries: A Practical Handbook*, Cambridge, MA, and Kidlington, UK: Chandos Publishing, 2018, https://doi.org/10.1016/B978-0-08-102107-1.00003-0

1. To reproduce the copyrighted work in copies or phonorecords
2. To prepare derivative works based upon the copyrighted work
3. To distribute copies or phonorecords of the copyrighted work to the public by sale or other transfer of ownership, or by rental, lease, or lending
4. In the case of literary, musical, dramatic, and choreographic works, pantomimes, and motion pictures and other audiovisual works, to perform the copyrighted work publicly
5. In the case of literary, musical, dramatic, and choreographic works, pantomimes, and pictorial, graphic, or sculptural works, including the individual images of a motion picture or other audiovisual work, to display the copyrighted work publicly
6. In the case of sound recordings, to perform the copyrighted work publicly by means of a digital audio transmission.

A very important point about copyright protection is that, in the United States, the work is under copyright protection from the moment it is created and fixed in a tangible form that is perceptible either directly or with the aid of a machine or device, also referred to as a tangible medium of expression. Registration is *not* required for a work to have copyright protection. Note, however, that registration does provide extra benefits to the copyright holder in case of infringement. Works are protected even though the work may not have the symbol © displayed.

Copyright law does not prohibit all copying or use of a work. For example, the fair use doctrine, codified by the Copyright Act of 1976 as 17 U.S.C. Section 107, permits some copying and distribution without permission of the copyright holder or payment to same. "Fair use" is not clearly defined in Section 107, and an in-depth discussion of fair use exceeds the scope of this book.

Trademarks. A trademark is a word, phrase, symbol or design, or a combination thereof that identifies and distinguishes the source of the goods or services of one party from those of others. Trademark protection does not prohibit all uses of the protected mark.

Trade Secrets. A trade secret is a formula, practice, process, design, instrument, pattern, or compilation of information that is not generally known or reasonably ascertainable, by which the owner of the trade secret can obtain an economic advantage. Trade secrets are often mentioned in confidentiality agreements.

When dealing with a license for intellectual property, the license must specify the following concepts:

1. **Exclusive vs. nonexclusive:** Does the license grant an exclusive or nonexclusive right to use the intellectual property?
   a) Very important: A grant of an exclusive license means that the person or entity granting the license ("licensor") can no longer use the intellectual property during the term of the license. For example, if a

university granted "Acme, Inc." the exclusive right to use one of the university's registered trademarks for five years, the university could not use the trademark for the five-year term. *Generally, all intellectual property grants from the university to others must be nonexclusive.*

b) If exclusivity is granted, the specific type of exclusivity must be addressed. In other words, exclusive rights to do what with the intellectual property.

2. **Term:** Is the license short term, long term, or perpetual? Note that a perpetual term would not mean until the end of time, but until the end of the life of the intellectual property rights. Further, a license can also be revocable (i.e., terminable by the license owner). See the next item.

3. **Revocability:** "Revocability" means the extent to which a license can be revoked (terminated) before its expiration date by the licensor. Contracts must specify whether a license is revocable and, if so, what steps must be taken and how much notice must be given to revoke the license.

4. **Geography:** "Geography" refers to geographic (territorial) restrictions on an intellectual property license. Does the license allow worldwide use of the intellectual property, or is the use limited to a certain region (e.g., North America)?

5. **Scope:** Scope relates to the extent to which and purposes for which the licensee may use the intellectual property. The specific scope must be mentioned in the contract. In other words, what use or uses are allowed by the licensee? For example, can the licensee make derivative works of a copyrighted work?

6. **Right to sublicense:** The license agreement must indicate whether or not the licensee has the right to further sublicense the rights given and, if so, what restrictions or terms govern such sublicenses.

7. **Quality control:** In trademark licenses, it is very important to include quality control provisions that give the university the right to monitor and control the licensee's use of the trademark. Failure to do so could result in a "naked license" that could undermine an organization's trademark rights.

Confidentiality Agreements

Confidentiality agreements are sometimes known as "nondisclosure agreements" (NDAs) or "confidential disclosure agreements" (CDAs).

If your organization will send its staff members to visit a company to provide training, there is a significant chance that the supplier will attempt to require your organization's staff to sign confidentiality agreements when the staff members arrive on the company's property.

Consider whether the confidentiality agreement is "one-way" or "two-way." A one-way confidentiality obligation only applies to one party, and a two-way obligation applies to both parties. Moreover, consider whether the confidentiality obligation lasts forever. If so, does that indefinite obligation make sense? And is it something your organization can comply with? If your organization is a public-sector organization, do public-records laws affect your ability to agree to confidentiality clauses? Does the agreement require you to destroy records at a certain point and, if so, does that sync with your organization's record-retention policies?

It is fairly common for licenses governing electronic resources to contain confidentially clauses. These clauses seek to require libraries to treat pricing as confidential information and prohibit them from disclosing this information to third parties. The restriction on sharing pricing information is detrimental to libraries in a number of ways. First, it greatly restricts libraries from comparing what they are paying to that of similar organizations and, as a result, prevents them from receiving more competitive pricing options. Second, confidentially clauses stand in stark contrast to the principle of transparency and the sharing of information that form the bedrock of librarianship. Lastly, it is extremely difficult to enforce confidentially agreements across entire organizations. Removing such clauses prevents a library from inadvertently violating the terms of an agreement.

Fortunately, many libraries and library organizations have pushed back against confidentially clauses in an attempt to move to a more open and competitive marketplace. As a result, many publishers are more comfortable removing confidentially clauses from agreements or rewording them in such a way that they only apply to trade secrets and not business terms such as price.

It is also worth mentioning that some libraries may be unable to agree to confidentially clauses due to public information laws. The authors therefore strongly recommend that all agreements with library vendors be edited to remove any confidentially clauses. Or in instances where legitimate concerns about trade secrets exist, such clauses should be edited to remove prohibitions on sharing business terms such as price.

Credit and Direct Bill Applications

Direct bill applications and credit applications are the same thing: vendors use both types of documents to obtain information about a customer to determine whether the customer is financially trustworthy to the point that the vendor is not taking an unnecessary risk by allowing the customer to pay after the vendor provides goods or services. Generally, direct bill applications are from hotels, and credit applications are for all other types of vendors.

Both types of documents are contracts. In the authors' experience, many organizations overlook direct bill and credit applications, and unfortunately, many organizations lack rules for how its staff must treat these documents. Failing to address direct bill and credit applications is risky because the documents tend to contain multiple problematic clauses, such as indemnity, collection costs, attorneys' fees, and so on. Moreover, virtually all direct bill and credit applications contain clauses that make the person signing the document personally liable for the costs of the goods or services that the vendor will provide as a result of the vendor approving the direct bill or credit application. Such clauses are called "personal guarantee" clauses. A personal guarantee is exactly what it sounds like: the person is guaranteeing the organization's creditworthiness.

Hotels

A common type of transaction for many organizations is when the organization contracts with a hotel to provide sleeping rooms, catering, meeting space, or any combination of those services. Although a hotel's business model is probably intuitive to most people, the hotel business model is worth noting because some end users might not stop to think about the issue. Needing to remind your end users about how hotels work is especially true if you work for a government agency. Many government employees take time to think through how their suppliers operate, but some do not (especially professors). Also, because government agencies do not have to make a profit, sometimes government employees tend to forget that businesses have to make a profit in order to survive. Hotels make money by selling space. The hotels lose money when space is not rented. If your organization contacts a hotel about any space (including sleeping rooms, meeting rooms, etc.), the hotel will hold that space as a courtesy for a certain period. While the hotel is holding the space for your organization, the hotel will likely have to turn away other potential business in order to hold the space for your organization. If your organization is a government agency, the hotel might offer CONUS (continental United States) rates. Although CONUS rates are typically not the lowest rate that a hotel offers, they are typically much lower than the hotel's usual rates.

In the authors' experience, many end users tend to book far more rooms or far too much space than they actually need. When end users book more space than they need, this situation creates issues for the hotel because the hotel will have empty space. Hotels typically allow attrition of up to 20%. Sometimes, hotels will allow a group coordinator to modify the sleeping room block by any amount without penalty.

If your organization is booking a room block with a hotel for a conference that your organization is hosting, most hotels will allow you to negotiate adding a commission fee/rebate for each sleeping room utilized under your organization's room block. This commission might be a firm dollar amount or a percentage. The firm dollar amount might be $3 to $5 per room, per night. This is the reason, by the way, why you might find that a hotel's "best available rate" (publicly available rate) is lower than a conference's room block.

Most hotels, like most suppliers, do not work with the government on a regular basis. Accordingly, the vast majority of hotels do not have special terms and conditions for government entities. Moreover, many hotels are not familiar with the reasons why government organizations must revise the hotel's terms. Also, hotels are not necessarily familiar with the budget constraints and processing delays. The typical processing delays in government organizations are particularly important to note to hotels. Most hotels will place a very short turnaround time/deadline on your organization getting a signed contract back to the hotel. A best practice would be for your organization to train end users to notify hotels of your organization's typical turnaround time. Also, a good practice is to "underpromise and overdeliver." In other words, estimate that the process will take longer than you believe it really will.

Hotels will usually send a standard contract to an organization for processing. These contracts generally contain the same issues, regardless of the specific hotel. A discussion of common issues that appear in hotel contracts follows.

Last-Room Availability. It is critical that any agreement with a hotel allow your organization to get the CONUS (or other agreed-upon rate) at "last-room availability." This means that the hotel will offer all rooms to your organization at the agreed-to rate.

Banquet Event Orders (BEOs) and Other Booking Forms. State that all BEOs and any other booking forms are governed by the contract between your organization and the hotel and that any additional terms do not apply to your organization.

Entire Transaction. Many hotels have different people in charge of the hotel's catering, audiovisual equipment, and rooms. Sometimes, every department in a hotel will have its own contract. It's very important that the contract documents contain the entire transaction.

Payment. It's important to determine who is paying for what charges. When contracting with hotels, entities have a few choices:

1. Individuals pay their own charges.
2. Individuals pay some charges; the group pays some charges.
3. Group pays all charges, except incidentals.

Itemized Charges. In order to make the accounts payable process easier for departments, it's important that the potential charges be listed.

Deadlines. A hotel's business model is based around booking rooms in the future. Hotels usually put super-short deadlines in their contracts (e.g., two to three days). In general, many organizations are poor communicators with hotels, and the hotels are not aware of an organization's rules or their contract routing/review procedures. Often, by the time the contract gets to the contract office, the hotel is already very frustrated. Contacting the hotel early and often via email will help keep the relationship on good terms.

Service Fees. Many times, hotel contracts will allow the hotel to increase the service fee at any time and without notice to an organization. For example:

- "[organization] will also pay the hotel service fee, currently 20%."
- "[organization] will also pay the hotel service fee, currently 20%—subject to change."

It is a best practice not to agree to unknown costs, so the service fees should be capped. Capping service fees so they do not exceed 20% is a good rule.

Force Majeure. Carefully review and consider force majeure language in hotel contracts. Many times, a hotel's force majeure clause will only apply to the hotel's ability to hold the event, and an organization will not have the ability to cancel without penalty due to force majeure. Because bad weather, natural disasters, terrorism, or other factors could cause the need to postpone or cancel an event, it's important that force majeure language give both parties the ability to cancel without penalty in the event that either party's performance is prevented due to a force majeure event.

Attrition. Attrition clauses guarantee that an organization spend a certain amount of money at the hotel—usually this applies to booked rooms. The industry standard is 80% of the contracted amount. Note that attrition fees can apply to booked rooms, meeting rooms, food and beverages, or audiovisual equipment. The key to understanding attrition clauses is that attrition kicks in when (1) the organization shows up and (2) the organization utilizes less than the guaranteed amount of rooms (or other goods/services) as specified in the contract.

If an organization fails to meet its attrition, the hotel will charge the difference of the number of rooms used and the attrition amount. Here are two examples:

- Example 1 (University owes attrition): A university department books 100 rooms, but only 70 people show up. The hotel's contract that the university signed contains an attrition clause stating that the university guarantees that it will utilize at least 80% of booked rooms. The hotel will charge the university for 10 additional rooms (70 + 10 = 80).
- Example 2 (University would not owe attrition): A university department books 100 rooms, and 80 people show up. The hotel's contract that the university signed contains an attrition clause stating that the university guarantees that it will utilize at least 80% of booked rooms. The university has met its 80% utilization requirement.

Example language:

Attrition:

a) Group room block (GRB): The [organization] and hotel will review GRB and meeting space 21 days prior to the event and, if necessary, the [organization] will make adjustments to the GRB and meeting space without penalty. This will be the cutoff date.

b) The [organization] will be responsible for a portion of nights not utilized on a cumulative basis below 80% of the total GRB after the cutoff date. This will be considered attrition damages, and these will be capped at 75% of the negotiated room rate, multiplied by the number of rooms below 80% of the GRB after the cutoff date. This amount shall be deemed to include all applicable service charges and taxes, and shall constitute full and complete settlement of any and all obligations that the [organization] may have in conjunction with attrition damages.

c) The GRB will be credited for any and all reservations made and used by the [organization] meeting attendees, regardless of the rate paid or method of booking, including all reservations made after the cutoff date.

d) If the hotel achieves occupancy levels above 90% on peak nights of a [organization] event, or if it becomes sold out on any night of a [organization] event, the [organization] will not be required to pay attrition damages.

e) If attrition damages are caused by one or more force majeure events, the [organization] will not be liable for attrition damages. Force majeure events include acts of God, war, government regulation; actual, threatened, or suspected terrorism; disaster; outbreak of disease in the surrounding area; strikes; civil disorder; curtailment of transportation; or any cause that makes it impossible for 25% of the attendees to attend the meeting. This would also include a threat of an imminent natural disaster that interferes with the hotel's operations or the ability of attendees to safely travel to [city hotel is located in]. Under any of these circumstances, it is agreed that the [organization] would not be liable for failure to meet GRB or food and beverage minimums for the event. The [organization] would be liable for actual services and food and beverages used.

f) For purposes of calculating attrition damages, the hotel will provide to the [organization\or its representative] within 30 days records reasonably required to substantiate any damages claimed by the hotel. The hotel general manager will certify that the records are complete and accurate.

Cancellation. Cancellation clauses are different from attrition because in order to "activate" a cancellation clause, an organization does not show up at all. Cancellation charges are usually based on the time between notice of cancellation to the hotel and the event. Following is an example cancellation structure that might appear in a hotel contract:

If [organization] cancels

- 100 or more days before event: 0%
- 99 to 60 days before the event: 50% of the contracted amount will be due
- 59 to 30 days before the event: 80% of the contracted amount will be due
- 29 days or less: 100% of the contracted amount will be due

Profit margins:
Sleeping rooms: 80%
Function space: 90%
Food and beverage (nonalcoholic): 30%
Alcohol: 80%
Audiovisual: 20%

Maintenance Agreements

When reviewing a maintenance agreement, think about the type of plan your organization is considering. Many times, salespeople will push your organization into buying the top-of-the-line coverage for an item (often, maintenance plans will have names such as "bronze," "silver," "gold," "platinum," etc.). Does your organization need the top-of-the-line coverage? For example, if the plan offers 24-hour coverage, is your organization even open 24 hours a day? Is the machine that critical to warrant more expensive coverage?

Also, can you obtain maintenance service through a third party? There are third-party services that provide maintenance coverage, such as the Remi Group. Often, these third-party services provide the same types of maintenance service at a reduced cost.

Catering

When reviewing catering agreements or agreements for catered meals at hotels, convention centers, and so on, you will likely find these agreements straightforward. The most important elements of a catering agreement are:

- Cancellation date
- Cutoff date to change the quantities you ordered
- The automatic overage that the caterer will prepare (for example, if your event is for 100 people, will the caterer prepare for 5% more, so 5 additional people at no charge?)
- Cancellation fees

How you negotiate catering agreements will probably depend on whether you are hiring a caterer to come to your property or you are having a catered meal at a hotel or event space. If you have the meal at a hotel or event space, you will be limited in your ability to select caterers. If the function is at a hotel, the hotel itself will usually prohibit outside food or beverages. If the function will be at an event space, most event spaces limit your choice of caterers. Having a limited pool of competition for catering will almost certainly cause your organization to pay more for the catering than you would if you have freedom in selecting the caterer.

In addition to negotiating more favorable pricing, if you have freedom in selecting caterers, you might be able to negotiate more favorable cancellation terms. Similar to hotels, caterers have limited capacity. Unlike hotels and sleeping rooms (which have limited space with no possibility to add capacity), many medium and large caterers have staff on an as-needed basis in addition to their regular full-time or part-time staff. Accordingly, caterers might have less to lose if your organization cancels the event.

Image Release/Property Release

Image releases (sometimes called "model releases") and releases for filming property are common, especially for government agencies. These agreements are typically straightforward, but be sure to remember that your organization (as property owner) has a lot of leverage against people who want to come to your property.

When it comes to individuals, sometimes if the other party provides your organization with a contract draft, the contract might contain a clause stating that the other party can photograph your employees and use those photographs for marketing or any other purposes. Unless your organization has documented its employees' consent to allow your organization to sign on their behalf when it comes to use of their name, likeness, and so on, your organization most likely does not have the legal ability to waive an individual's right to privacy. If your organization does not have the right to sign on behalf of individual employees, be sure to tell the other party that it must secure each individual's consent to being photographed.

Performers, Speakers, Lecturers, and Others

Contracts with performers, speakers, and lecturers tend to follow one of two formats: your organization enters into a contract with the individual themselves, or your organization enters into a contract with a management company or third-party representative of the performer, speaker, or lecturer.

Often, contracts with performers, speakers, and lecturers include a clause prohibiting anyone from recording the performance, speech, or lecture. Although such clauses are most likely legally permissible, consider three key things:

- Does your organization have legal control over everyone who will attend? If not, then you need to consider the clause very carefully. If third parties will attend (such as students, members of the public, etc.), the best practice would be to modify the clause prohibiting recording to state that your organization will use reasonable efforts to prevent recording, but remove any language that makes your organization liable for damages if someone records the event.

- What steps can your organization take to prevent recording? Will your organization make announcements, post signs, or do something similar? Does the prohibition of recording apply to your organization's security systems?

- What happens if someone records the event? A good practice would be to specify in the contract what will happen. For example, if a member of the public attends and your organization catches the person recording, your organization's obligation might be to ask the person to stop on the first violation, confiscate the recording device, or even escort the person out of the event. Your organization might even consider obtaining a device to stop phones or other recording devices from being used, such as Yondr.[1]

Because recording devices are common, easily concealed, and nearly ubiquitous and technically include things such as security cameras, carefully consider contractual clauses regarding recording.

Many performers and speakers tend to have "riders" with their contracts. The band Van Halen made these riders famous.[2] The band used riders as a proverbial "canary in the coal mine": the band required their stage to hold a certain amount of weight due to the band's equipment. A stage that was not sturdy enough to hold a certain amount of weight posed a serious safety problem for the band. To help ensure that the host venue read their rider, the band included a clause requiring the venue to place a bowl of M&M candy in the band's dressing room, but the venue had to remove all of the brown M&Ms. If the band saw that the brown M&Ms were in the candy bowl, the band refused to perform, because the band assumed that the venue's managers had not read the rider at all.[3]

Please remember the Van Halen story, and please always carefully read riders. The riders often contain important information related to technical requirements (such as electricity, sound requirements, etc.), logistics, and so on. Sometimes, the riders contain potentially controversial items, such as the performer or speaker asking for alcohol, expensive food or beverage items, candles (consider the risk of an open flame indoors), or something similar.

Often, organizations will process contracts with other service providers that are related to the performer's, speaker's, or lecturer's contract—for example, catering hotels for a room block, equipment rental, and so on. What will happen if the speaker, performer, or lecturer is unable to show up to the event? Will your organization be able to reschedule or cancel those other contracts without paying fees? Do not rely on a generic force majeure clause to save your organization from cancellation fees or other liquidated damages if the speaker, performer, or lecturer cancels. If you want the ability to cancel without fees if the speaker, performer, or lecturer cannot make it to the event, the best practice would be to state that explicitly in contracts that are related to the event, such as hotels, catering, equipment rental, and so on. Many companies will probably not agree to allow your organization to cancel outright without fees, even if the performer, speaker, or lecturer is unable to attend the event.

Residential Leases for the Benefit of Students or Employees

When negotiating a lease for the benefit of students or employees, be sure to closely review your state's landlord and tenant laws to ensure that your lease complies with those laws, if applicable. In addition to reviewing and accounting for the typical clauses in a residential lease (move-in date, stay-over, etc.), you will need to consider very carefully the damages, utilities, and other clauses. If your organization is going to pay the landlord for rent and utilities, what happens if the students damage the facility? Will utilities be included in the rent? If so, what happens if a student fails to report a leaking faucet, toilet, or something else and the water bill for a given month is much higher than usual? How will the landlord capture the students' or employees' agreement to the landlord's rules and regulations?

Another very real concern is if your organization will have the right to enter the residential units. If so, your organization must develop a protocol with the landlord and establish a list of names of people authorized to enter the residential units. The reason is to prevent an abusive staff member from entering the property—at least, the goal is to minimize such an occurrence. Moreover, determine whether your organization needs to notify each resident before your organization enters a unit.

If your organization has an internal housing program where students or employees stay in property owned and managed by your organization, the best practice would be to establish an emergency plan in case of fire, flood, mold, infestation, and so on. Consider prequalifying local apartment complexes and negotiating the terms of your lease agreement in advance of the possible emergency use. Consider also what other services you might need in the event of a major emergency: movers, dry cleaners, property cleaners, disaster cleanup experts, pest control, mold remediation, and so on, and have a plan in place for which vendors you will contact in the event of any foreseeable emergency.

Public Records

If your business is a public-sector entity, your business is probably subject to a public records law. Public records laws (sometimes referred to as "open records" laws) vary in applicability. Some states maintain public records laws that make records open to anyone, whereas other states limit applicability to residents of the particular state. For example, Tennessee's public records law limits its applicability to Tennessee residents.

Public records laws also vary in scope. Some states maintain public records laws that limit the laws' respective scope to certain types of records, whereas other states maintain very broad public records laws. For example, Tennessee's public records law has a very broad scope, and it applies to most records that a Tennessee government agency maintains.

Public records laws are important to consider when you establish processes for contract review. Even if your organization is not subject to public records laws, perhaps consider whether you need to establish processes to deal with sensitive information in contracts, such as Social Security numbers, bank account numbers, personally identifiable health information, and so on.

When you redact, consider how you redact. Adobe's redaction tool is effective and very easy to use. When you redact something, you can redact using black or white.

CONCLUSION

Although your organization might not encounter all of the types of clauses discussed here on a regular basis, it is helpful to understand these clauses so that you are prepared. In the next chapter, we will consider common circumstances that arise when dealing with contracts, such as documenting internal organizational approvals.

NOTES

1. See Yondr's website for more details, https://www.overyondr.com/
2. This American Life, "Fine Print," https://www.thisamericanlife.org/386/fine-print (cited March 4, 2019).
3. This American Life, "Fine Print."

5

Administering Contracts

INTRODUCTION

Generally speaking, there are no absolute right or wrong ways to organize or manage a contract. In this chapter, we will provide a high-level discussion regarding contract layout and suggestions for managing contracts. We will discuss how templates can be used to create more efficient and understandable licenses. Furthermore, we will provide tips for negotiating contractual sticking points and provide a possible way to find a path forward when institutional roadblocks are present. Finally, we will discuss a best practice for terminating a contract.

CONTRACT ORGANIZATION

Please note that we believe using your own license template is the most efficient way to organize a license, as it allows you to control the flow of the document. As such, we provide guidance for your organization's templates in this chapter. We fully recognize, however, that there will be times when using your own template will not be possible. In these cases, we recommend that you avoid trying to rearrange contracts from another party. Instead, when encountering another party's draft, the best practice is to avoid changing the other party's format, language, and so on if your reason for changing is only stylistic.[1]

We recommend that you structure your organization's templates in the same format so that each document has the same "look and feel." We further recommend that you create a document that contains all of your organization's standard clauses so that you can use that document as the central source of all contract language for your organization. This tactic will make all of your contracts look the same and contain the same substantive clauses.

Be sure to schedule time each year to review your templates and the central document that contains your organization's standard clauses. Reviewing quarterly or twice per year would be optimal. Consider scheduling a routine meeting with applicable stakeholders every quarter or every six months to discuss the templates and standard clauses. Your goal in reviewing the templates and standard clauses regularly is to ensure that the language is current, accurate, and meets your organization's needs.

Suggested model layout:
1. Title (in the header of your document)
2. Introductory clause
3. Recitals (if needed)
4. Lead-in/language of agreement ("the parties agree as follows")
5. Body
6. Signature blocks
7. Schedules[2] (if applicable)
8. Exhibits[3] (if applicable)

Title

Be sure to use Microsoft Word's header area for your contract's first page. In Word, you may access the header by double-clicking at the top of the first page or going to the Insert tab and clicking Header. Unless you want the title to appear on each page, be sure to click "Different First Page" *before* you start typing. The standard practice is to place the title in the center of the header. Consider using either all capital letters for the title[4] or bold text and capitalize each word of the title. Also consider whether avoiding all capital letters in the title would improve readability. Generally speaking, most drafters use the word "agreement" in the title instead of "contract."[5]

Introductory Clause

Here is a short list of what should *not* be in the introductory clause:

- Capital "A" in "this Agreement": Although the practice is very common, you do not need to refer to the contract itself as a proper noun (i.e., "this Agreement"). There is no point, or even sense, in making the word "agreement" a proper noun because "this agreement" is clear.[6]
- An outdated phrase: Although the phrase is becoming less common, sometimes some drafters include the phrase "know all men by these presents." Including this phrase is unnecessary and outdated.[7]
- Any substantive provisions: Keep substantive phrases in the body of your contract.

- Any recitals: Keep any recitals in their own section.
- "By and between": This phrase is an unnecessary couplet, and although the phrase is common, it is not necessary.[8] Simply use "between" instead.
- The word "consideration:" see *A Manual of Style for Contract Drafting, Fourth Edition* (MSCD) for more details on why you do not need to refer to the existence of consideration in your contract, generally, or the introductory clause, in particular.[9]
- "Now, therefore": This phrase is outdated and not necessary.[10]

What should be in the introductory clause:

- Date: Including a date in the introductory clause can be a useful way to date the contract generally. The date can be used in the future if you amend the contract (the amendment can easily reference the date, for example, "the License Agreement dated January 25, 2020"). For a more in-depth discussion on dates, please see MSCD 2.23 to 2.45.
- Names of the parties: Give each party a short name, and make the short name a defined term. For example: "The University of Tennessee, an instrumentality of the state of Tennessee ("University") . . .". To make the agreement more readable, and to avoid confusion,[11] refrain from using similar terms for each party (for example, "Licensor" paired with "Licensee").[12]
- Legal nature of the parties: Be sure to describe the legal nature of each party. For example, state if the party is a Delaware corporation or an instrumentality of the state of Nevada.

Sample introductory clause with header showing:

Digital Content License Agreement

This digital content license agreement is dated January 1, 2025, and is between Fiona Content Corporation, a Nevada Corporation ("Licensor"), and The University of Desert, an instrumentality of the state of New Mexico ("University").

Recitals

Consider whether you need to use recitals at all. Simple contracts almost certainly do not benefit from recitals, and in the case of a simple contract, including recitals unnecessarily adds length to the document. If you include recitals, do not use the archaic words "Witnesseth" or "Whereas."[13] Consider giving the recitals section a heading, such as "Recitals" or "Background."[14]

Lead-in

Simply say, "The parties agree as follows:" [Note: This is the only place in the contract where the word "agree" appears. There is no need to use the words "agree," "agrees," etc., in other parts of the contract.] In other words, the concept of the parties agreeing to the contract should appear only once: in the lead-in.[15]

Body

Consider including language that is not specific to the transaction in the body (for example, governing law, etc.). Using that approach makes it easier for your contract-administration staff to complete your templates. If you use this approach, you would include the transaction-specific clauses to a schedule. For an authoritative look at categories of contract language, we recommend you review Chapter 3 of the MSCD.

Signature Blocks

The parties are signing this agreement on the date stated in the introductory clause.[16]

Party	**Party**
Signature: _____	Signature: _____
Name: _____	Name: _____
Title: _____	Title: _____

Attachments

Attachments might be called any number of things: addendum, annex, annexure, appendix, attachment, exhibit, schedule, and so on. We recommend following the MSCD's view that you call attachments one or two names, depending on their purpose: "schedules" are documents that contain transaction-specific information, and "exhibits" are stand-alone documents.[17] You should avoid putting any contract sections in schedules,[18] unless your schedules include the entire transaction-specific set of clauses.

Be sure to maintain consistency when you have attachments. Refer to attachments as:

Exhibit: A stand-alone document.

Schedule: Schedules consist of materials that could be included in the body of the contract but instead have been moved to after the signature blocks. Moving content to schedules might be useful when the content is complicated, highly technical, or similar. Also, moving content to a schedule ensures that the main contract document's formatting does not change.

As with any process, being consistent is important. The authors recommend that you follow MSCD: Do *not* refer to attachments as anything else.[19] Examples of what *not* to call attachments include:

Addendum
Amendments
Annex
Appendix
Attachment

NEGOTIATING

Contract management is just as important as contract review and organization. The more contracts that your organization has, the harder it will be to manage them. Negotiating contracts involves not only negotiating business terms such as price, coverage dates, and usage rights but also negotiating general terms, such as indemnification and governing law. Because the negotiation process will result in what the final contract looks like, it is important to understand how the negotiation process works and how to maximize your leverage to ensure the best possible outcomes.

When negotiating a contract, it can be useful to think of it in two separate pieces. The first piece deals with nonbusiness terms that are either negotiable or non-negotiable. For example, if your organization has sovereign immunity, giving that up is non-negotiable. On the other hand, you may have some wiggle room negotiating language concerning governing law.

The second piece deals with business terms and, generally speaking, is where the majority of tension in a negotiation will occur. Business terms include anything that isn't codified by law, policies, or procedures. In other words, they are the things where you have the most wiggle room and, consequently, the most amount of leverage. These are also the items that many people worry about messing up during a negotiation. Our advice is not to worry so much about them, because although contract negotiation can be intimidating, there are some broadly applicable practices that will help improve your contract negotiation skills and confidence levels. And if you prepare for the negotiation and approach the process systematically, you can ensure a relatively smooth process.

Before we mention specific strategies, it's important to mention that if your organization is a government entity, unless you notify or remind them, a vendor will most likely assume that your entity is a private company. When dealing with a vendor, you might find the following steps helpful in establishing at the outset that the negotiation will take place between a government entity and private company.

The very first step in any contract-review process should be for your organization to obtain a copy of the contract so that a thorough review can be completed. It is usually at this point that you will want to notify the other party that your organization is a government entity. Although not very common, some vendors maintain separate agreement templates for government entities, and those government-entity templates often do not contain clauses that are essentially universally problematic for government entities, such as indemnification. It is worth your time to ask the vendor explicitly whether the vendor has a separate set of terms for governmental agencies. In other words, do not rely on the vendor "connecting the dots" between you informing the vendor that your organization is a government agency and the vendor realizing that they need to provide a separate set of terms for you. If the vendor does not have standard terms and conditions for government entities, it is often helpful to ask how they deal with other government entities. Note that this tactic can be a double-edged sword, however, because the vendor might respond by claiming that no other organization has ever requested revisions to the vendor's agreement.

The second step in negotiating a contract is to conduct research to see what, if any, concessions the vendor has allowed when it comes to editing an agreement. Consider using public records requests to obtain copies of contracts between the vendor and other government agencies to see what changes the vendor accepted. If the vendor has primarily worked with private organizations, you may try and leverage connections through professional associations to gather intelligence. While the legal concept of "precedent" does not apply outside of the courtroom, pointing out to a vendor that they agreed to make certain changes for a similarly situated party can be a strong negotiation point. After all, if the vendor agreed to it once before, there is likely no legal reason prohibiting the vendor from agreeing again.

After you have conducted your research, you should make any necessary or desired changes to the agreement and begin the actual negotiating process. Whether you are a government agency or not, you can gain efficiencies by approaching negotiating your contract revisions in a disciplined way. The authors highly recommend using Word's tracked changes feature when making revisions and Word's comment feature to explain your revisions. If you are unfamiliar with Word, many free and high-quality training videos are available on the Internet. Although it may be tempting to use the "lock" feature in Word, the authors recommend against locking tracked changes because doing so provides a false sense of security. It is extremely easy to unlock a locked Word document by following steps obtained by a simple Internet search. It is better to keep things open and editable to ensure you do not miss any edits.

Two of the worst possible ways to revise a contract are to (1) fail to use tracked changes and (2) fail to explain your organization's revisions. Doing either—or worse, both—will virtually guarantee that you frustrate the other party. Moreover, doing either tactic will guarantee a longer time spent negotiating the contract and delay the outcome you're trying to achieve. To ensure that edits and the reasons behind them are clear, you should use tracked changes and explain every edit. The authors suggest the following format for explaining revisions:

Cite the legal, policy, or business reason for the change.
Explain the available options.
Inform the vendor whether this issue is a deal-breaker or if it is negotiable. If the issue is a deal-breaker, it is best to be explicit.

To help take your organization to the next level of contract negotiation, we recommend that you create a document containing template responses for common changes. This will not only make your organization consistent when it explains changes to contracts, it will also improve the efficiency of your contract-review staff members.

The following are some basic considerations when negotiating contract terms:

1. Before you begin the negotiations:
   a) Determine what options you have. If you can walk away from a vendor, you have much more leverage. If you cannot walk away, you have significantly less leverage. Even if it appears that you do not have leverage, you always have at least some leverage. This can be difficult for libraries that rely on certain products to support research or support a community. No product should be so essential to libraries, though, that they cannot walk away from a bad deal that has the potential to damage a library through serious financial hardship or open it to possible litigation. Because of this, the authors recommend two things. First, constantly be on the lookout for materials that can compete with or replace existing materials. Second, keep your users and/or governing bodies informed of the issues you are facing. For example, although faculty members might be less than thrilled that a journal subscription needs to be cancelled, they will be more understanding if you offer an explanation why (cost, accessibility issues opening the institution up to litigation, etc.) and offer an alternative for their use.
   b) Determine who will negotiate for your organization. You want to speak with "one voice" to avoid confusing the vendor and to minimize the risk that someone within your entity will accidentally undermine your negotiation. This does not mean that a team approach to negotiation should not be used behind the scenes, however. In fact, most vendors have several people working on negotiations, whereas most libraries have one or two people, at best. The authors recommend building a team of subject matter experts who can review and provide feedback on licensing terms. The team, however, should designate a spokesperson who acts as the point of contact with the other party throughout the entire negotiation. This will allow the library to maximize talent while mitigating the risk of a misunderstanding occurring. It is worth noting

that the spokesperson for the team need not be the team leader. Instead, the team should play to its strengths for maximum effect. If the senior team member is super talented at drafting alternative language but gets easily flustered when speaking with a vendor, it is a better idea to let someone else be the "face and voice" of the negotiating team.

2. You should never include end users in the contract terms and conditions negotiation process. The further removed the end users are from the process, the smoother the negotiation will go. End users just want to get their jobs done, and if they are involved, they might panic when they see the parties negotiating, especially if the vendor postures and threatens to cancel an event, raise a price, or something similar. However, this does not mean that negotiating teams should not solicit feedback from end users before the process begins. In fact, the contrary should occur. Libraries should maintain a healthy cycle of assessment that provides critical feedback of resources both before and after a purchase is made. This will ensure that time is spent negotiating purchases or renewals that bring value to an organization.

3. When reviewing contracts, it is very helpful if you include *all* of the comments and changes in the draft that the vendor sees the first time. In other words, the contract should go through the entire appropriate review process at your organization (all stakeholders, all levels of review) before the vendor sees any comments or red-lines. If you are going to use a team approach to negotiating—which you should—then it will be important to track versions as they move between each team member. This will be significantly easier to do if your organization uses contract-management software. If you do not have access to contract-management software, you can still be successful by establishing some simple guidelines involving file-naming conventions or utilizing collaborative software such as Google Docs.

4. As noted earlier, explain every single change (except for obvious ones, such as correcting a misspelled word). Your goal is to eliminate prolonged negotiations. The clearer you explain your changes, the less likely you are to be stuck exchanging needles emails, or worse, engaging in phone-based negotiations. Phone calls are inherently inefficient, if for no other reason than the issues involved in scheduling.

5. If possible, it is best to make changes in an electronic file. Earlier, we assumed that you would have access to Word files. If the vendor did not provide you with Word files, you should ask for a copy in Word. If the vendor refuses, try to obtain an original PDF and then covert it to Word. Working with the electronic file will have several benefits, including:

   a) If you save it, you can use it next time you deal with the vendor.

   b) By eliminating the need to initial changes, the document will be cleaner and neater.

   c) It improves the legibility of documents for scanning purposes.

6. Once both parties agree on changes, include the mutually agreed changes in a final draft. The final version must be clean: eliminate the need to initial revisions.

7. Neither party should sign until the document is in final (mutually agreed upon) form. Each party should only sign the document once (eliminate the need for any party to sign more than once, including initials). Initialing every page creates unnecessary work and adds no value to the contract-review process.

Either by your initial Word comment or via separate email, you should explain the overarching reasons why you made changes to a contract. For example, here is an overarching explanation that The University of Tennessee uses:

Please note that the university made several modifications to the agreement. The University of Tennessee is a state-created public institution of higher education. As an Instrumentality of the State of Tennessee, the university has sovereign immunity under Article I, Section 17 of the Tennessee Constitution and the Eleventh Amendment to the Constitution of the United States. Only the Tennessee General Assembly has authority to waive sovereign immunity; no officials at the university have this authority. Additionally, the university has limited contracting authority and can agree only to contract terms that are consistent with Tennessee law.

Sample email (Be sure to modify the email to meet your needs):

Dear [name]:

Good [morning/afternoon/evening]. My name is [fill in your name], and I am [title] at [legal name of your organization]. I am contacting you because I was asked to review the attached contract. Please find attached a copy of [the redlined agreement/agreement with changes, etc.].

Please note that [the entity—your employer] made several modifications to the agreement. [Explain the legal nature of your entity and what laws or regulations affect its ability to agree to contract terms.]

[Below, In the attached, etc.], I have provided explanations for my revisions. These explanations are offered solely to provide you a brief explanation of the basis underlying certain contract changes. They are not intended as, and must not be relied upon as, legal advice.

Please let me know if you have questions or need additional information. I look forward to hearing from you.

Thank you,

[Name of contract office employee]
[title]
[email, phone #, etc.]

DATA ENTRY AND SOFTWARE

The authors have not conducted a formal study on this topic, but have informally discussed the issue of contract management with several peers. Based on those discussions, institutions vary dramatically. Some institutions use Microsoft Excel spreadsheets, whereas others might use no tracking methods, and others use sophisticated software.

In an ideal situation, your institution will have a software system that captures the following:

- Basic data about the contract
- Renewal dates and expirations
- Cycle times throughout the review cycle
- Workflow stops
- Digital copies of the draft contract, the final version, the fully signed contract, and more
- Related documents, such as insurance certificates, licenses, and similar, along with the documents' respective expiration dates

In the event that your organization does not have access to software management, you can use any number of project management or commonly found software to keep track of the negotiation process. Although not as simple as using contract-management software, when coupled with some decision-making tools, they can be quite effective, if not too cumbersome.

For example, the Acquisitions and Continuing Resources Department at The University of Tennessee Libraries used a combination of a Word document, an Excel spreadsheet, and a Kepner-Tregoe Matrix (see Figure 5.1)—all stored on a shared drive to track potential purchases through the negotiation lifecycle. The shared Word document was used as the master version of the agreement, and individuals updated it as needed to reflect desired changes. Each team member tracked their assigned tasks using the Excel spreadsheet and updated it as tasks were completed. Lastly, the Kepner-Tregoe Matrix was updated by the lead negotiator as concessions were made by each party.

			Decision Matrix for: Scientific Journals Package					
Must Have	≤ 5% increase cap (yes/no)		Yes		Yes		Yes	Yes
	WCAG 2.0 Compliant (yes/no)		No		Yes		Yes	Yes
			Vendor A		Vendor B		Vendor C	Vendor D
		Weight	Rating	Score	Rating	Score	Rating	Score	Rating	Score
Like to Have	ILL lending privileges	2	x	x	2	4	4	6	1	3
	15% title swap allowance	3	x	x	2	5	2	5	3	8
	90 day cancellation	2	x	x	0	2	1	3	3	6
			Total A	0	Total B	11	Total C	14	Total D	17
			Weight + Rating = Score						
			Weight Scale		Rating Scale				
			1 - Least Important		0 - No Fit				
			2 - Moderately Important		1 - Low Fit				
			3 - Important		2 - Fit				
			4 - Very Important		3 - Good Fit				
			5 - Extremely Important		4 - Perfect Fit				

In another example, the State University of New York Maritime College Library used the project management software Basecamp to track the contract review and negotiation process. The negotiation team leader assigned tasks to individuals and uploaded the necessary documents. In this particular instance, only one individual was assigned to update the actual agreements, so there was no need to enable shared editing of documents. Instead, individuals focused more on either reviewing and commenting on specific sections or working closely with departments external to the library to ensure compliance with existing policies and procedures.

EXCEPTION MEMOS

If your organization has policies or other official rules governing contracts, the best practice is to determine which rules are based on state law and which are not. Many organizations develop "urban legends" about where rules came from and why they exist. The authors recommend carefully reviewing your organization's policies and procedures on a regular basis (for example, annually) and determining the source of all policies and procedures.

If your organization allows for flexibility with contract revisions, consider developing a memo that will allow your organization to document when deviations from standard policy occur. It is important to record both what occurred and why. In the authors' experience, this type of memo is known as an "exception" memo, because the memo details why the organization deviated from (took an exception to) its basic policy. Also, determine who has approval within your organization to make exceptions to its official policies.

A sample exception memo follows:

From: [your name]
To: [officials with power to grant exceptions to your organization's policies]
CC: [other stakeholders, such as the legal office or internal audit]
Date: [date]
RE: [quick explanation of what the exception request covers]

[In the body of the memo, describe:]

   Background (nature of the pending transaction, why your organization
      needs this good or service, etc.)
   Attempts to negotiate with the vendor
   What the vendor agreed to change
   What the vendor refused to change and why
   Why the final version deviates from your organization's policy and what
      risks arise as a result

Here is an example of an exception memo:

From: Blake Reagan
To: Corey Halaychik
Date: January 2, 2030
RE: Exception request for University of Cats contract

As you know, our university has been in contract negotiations with the University of Cats since last spring. The purpose of the contract is to enter into an affiliation agreement between our two institutions.

Unfortunately, the University of Cats has no legal flexibility on areas important to our university, the University of Dogs.

First, the University of Cats cannot legally agree to buy insurance. The University of Cats' contract representative, Fiona Reagan, advised that the University of Cats is covered by a self-insurance program, which covers the University of Cats for up to nine times actual damages. The University of Dogs' contracts policy (Dog Policy 7, Section 9) requires other parties to maintain commercial insurance at levels specified in the University of Dogs' risk management manual.

Second, the University of Cats cannot agree to confidentiality clauses. The state of Cats has enacted a law prohibiting all state agencies in the state of Cats from agreeing to confidentiality clauses. See Cats Code Annotated 19-1-103.

All other changes to the terms of the contract are mutually acceptable, and University of Dogs Fiscal Policy 1 provides you with the authority to waive any requirements stated in other fiscal policies. Please let me know if you have questions.

TERMINATIONS

When your organization decides to consider terminating a contract, be sure to review the contract carefully. In particular, review the contract's term section, termination section, liquidated damages section (if applicable), and (perhaps most importantly) the notices section. It is not uncommon for vendors to require that libraries provide 90- or 60-day notices when cancelling subscriptions. Libraries therefore need to be especially mindful of termination notification dates and work to ensure that decisions about retention or cancellation occur well before the cancellation period expires. Libraries should also be mindful of any clauses in agreements that allow for the archival of previously subscribed to or purchased content. If such archiving privileges exist, it is recommended that they be referenced along with specific titles in the cancellation letter.

When terminating a contract, your organization needs to consider at least the following:

- Have the appropriate stakeholders provided input on whether to terminate the contract?
- Why are you terminating? For cause (other party breached) or for other reasons?
- Are other transactions, whether formal contracts or otherwise, tied to the contract that you're terminating? If so, are you able to terminate those transactions?
- Who is responsible for sending the notice of cancellation?
- Have plans been made to notify end users that a resource will no longer be available? And, if applicable, have alternative resources been identified?
- When will the removal of any links to resource or removing/suppressing catalog records occur?
- Has the agreement been reviewed to see if archival privileges apply and, if so, have arrangements been made to facilitate the process?
- Are you sending the cancellation notice to the correct address and in the correct format?
- How will you verify that the cancellation letter has been received by the vendor?

Sample letter:

[vendor address] [be sure to send the letter exactly as stated in the contract's notice provision; if the contract lacks a notice provision, send via certified mail with return receipt requested and also send via email]

[date]

To [vendor name]:

[Name of your organization] hereby exercises its right to [terminate or nonrenew] the following [contract or contracts]: [list contract(s) and include the effective date for each contract].
[Describe the section of each contract that allows your organization to terminate or nonrenew.] [Describe the effective date of termination.] [Describe your organization's obligations after delivering the termination notice.]
[If your organization owes the other party money, describe when your organization will pay the other party.]
[If the other party owes your organization money or a deliverable, state this in the letter and provide a deadline.]

[If termination is for cause, list the steps that your organization followed to notify the other party of the other party's breach, and describe the opportunities your organization gave the other party to cure this.]

Please let me know if you have any questions.

Thank you,

[signature of authorized official]

[name of authorized official]

CONCLUSION

When it comes to organization and managing contracts, it pays to invest time at the beginning to consider how you want to structure a license and how you will handle negotiating its contents. Creating license templates will greatly speed up the review process. Furthermore, templates allow you to ensure that the terms most important to your organization are always included. This, in turn, helps with negotiations, as it allows the other party to see everything your organization is asking for at the beginning of the process.

Unfortunately, even well-written templates and expert negotiations may still hit institutional roadblocks from time to time. In these cases, it may be useful to seek an exception, and this chapter has provided a boilerplate for creating your own exception letter. Moreover, because all things must eventually end, the chapter provides a sample termination letter, which can be adapted to your institutional needs. Using a professional letter will ensure your organization properly informs a vendor of the agreement's termination in a way that preserves the business relationship for possible future endeavors.

NOTES

1. Adams, Kenneth A., *A Manual of Style for Contract Drafting* (4th ed.), p. xxxix.
2. Adams, *A Manual of Style for Contract Drafting*, p. 161, section 5.76.
3. Adams, *A Manual of Style for Contract Drafting*, p. 161, section 5.76.
4. Adams, *A Manual of Style for Contract Drafting*, p. 14, section 2.2.
5. Adams, *A Manual of Style for Contract Drafting*, p. 12, section 2.11.
6. Adams, *A Manual of Style for Contract Drafting*, p. 30, sections 2.124–2.128.
7. Adams, *A Manual of Style for Contract Drafting*, p. 13, section 2.16.
8. Adams, *A Manual of Style for Contract Drafting*, p. 6, 18, sections 1.38, 2.48–2.50.

9. Adams, *A Manual of Style for Contract Drafting*, pp. 36–41, sections 2.166–2.210.
10. Adams, *A Manual of Style for Contract Drafting*, p. 36, section 2.167.
11. Adams, *A Manual of Style for Contract Drafting*, p. 26, section 2.105.
12. Adams, *A Manual of Style for Contract Drafting*, pp. 26–28, sections 2.105–2.109.
13. Adams, *A Manual of Style for Contract Drafting*, p. 32, sections 2.137–2.140.
14. Adams, *A Manual of Style for Contract Drafting*, p. 32, section 2.139.
15. Adams, *A Manual of Style for Contract Drafting*, p. 51, section 3.30.
16. Adams, *A Manual of Style for Contract Drafting*, pp. 150–152, sections 5.8–5.20.
17. Adams, *A Manual of Style for Contract Drafting*, pp. 163–165, sections 5.94–5.105.
18. Adams, *A Manual of Style for Contract Drafting*, p. 164, section 5.101.
19. Adams, *A Manual of Style for Contract Drafting*, p. 161, sections 5.76–5.77.

6

Conclusion

The book you just read represents an attempt to help you, the reader, rapidly learn the tools and techniques that it took the authors years of experience and the occasional mistake (or two) to develop. Neither of the authors were able to find such a resource when they first started in careers that required contract review, and we hope this book provides you with a strong foundation and introduction to contract review.

We recognize that our hope—to provide you with strong foundational knowledge—is daunting, given the complexity of contracts. Furthermore, we acknowledge that many people, be they just starting out or seasoned contract reviewers, can be overwhelmed by legalese. For these reasons, we have provided information in a conversational tone as a way to reinforce the recommendation we make in the book about using clear and simple language in contracts as a way to remove ambiguity.

You may have also noticed that the book relies on practical solutions and real-world examples to illustrate our points. As practitioners, the authors do not have the luxury to ponder and debate the finer points of contract drafting. Instead, we must face the realities of working in university systems with multiple layers of bureaucracy, restrictive policies, and limited resources. The authors use all of the tools and advice included in the book on a regular basis to negotiate, organize, and review contracts. We assume that you, too, encounter some or all of these things in your professional work, and we have therefore included only practical tools and solutions as a way to help you navigate the issues you encounter in an effective and efficient way.

Lastly, the authors recognize that both libraries and the legal environment are consistently changing, and the last thing we wanted to do was write a book that would be out of date before it hit the shelves. We also recognize, though, that there is truth in the old adage "the more things change, the more they stay the same." With this in mind, we were intentional in providing you with actionable information that will allow you to implement changes now but will also still be useful for many years to come.

Appendix A

Contract Review Checklist

The following is a checklist that the University of Tennessee's System Administration Office of Procurement Services uses. The checklist is not an official university document. Because each organization's contract rules will vary substantially, the authors did not attempt to make this checklist generally applicable. Rather, the purpose of this checklist is to provide a starting point for creating your own checklist.

Contract Review Checklist			
Last updated: 10/31/2018			
Version: 3.7			
Contract number:			
My name:			
Delegated or Non-Delegated:			

Checklist always required, except use is optional when reviewing contracts with: other government agencies; UT standard template; approved template on UT's contract website.

ESM Contract Entry and Attachments

	ESM Data	Initials or "N/A"	Date
	All data entered in ESM matches the contract document (for example, dates in the actual contract match the dates in ESM). Make corrections as needed.		
	ESM "contract title" field is a stand-alone explanation of the contract and contains sufficient detail. Example of unacceptable title: "hotel contract." Example of acceptable title: "Hotel for UT Extension directors' meeting in Nashville, April 2018."		

	Contract Type	Initials or "N/A"	Date
	If the contract involves UT paying the contractor at all (including when the transaction is a net-revenue contract), ensure that the contract type is "Payable."		

	Revised Drafts	Initials or "N/A"	Date
	Be sure to upload the latest version of the red-lined contract (Word or PDF), with changes and comments.		

Remove Unnecessary (including Superseded) Attachments	Initials or "N/A"	Date
Be sure to remove any unnecessary attachments, such as superseded versions of draft contracts.		

Approval Emails	Initials or "N/A"	Date
Upload any related email approvals, such as Office of General Counsel; Audit; AP; Tax, etc.		

Approval Notes	Initials or "N/A"	Date
Be sure to use the "approval notes" field to include the latest updates to keep all stakeholders and coworkers informed. Specifically, be sure to include updates on when you correspond with: General Counsel; Controller's Office; Licensing; or the vendor.		

Process

Queue guidelines	Initials or "N/A"	Date
I am in compliance with SOP 12		
I am not in compliance with SOP 12. I have notified the associate director.		

Attachments	Initials or "N/A"	Date
If the contract references attachments (often called "addendum," "attachment," "appendix," "exhibit," or "schedule"), all referenced attachments are attached to the contract.		

	Receivable Contract?	Initials or "N/A"	Date
	Is contract receivable?		
	Yes (if yes, send to [named person or title] in the Controller's Office)		
	No		

	Payable Contract?	Initials or "N/A"	Date
	Is contract payable?		
	Yes		
	I have reviewed the "Payable Agreements" section of the manual and made all appropriate changes.		
	I have discussed any concerns about AP issues with [named person or title].		
	Add UT's standard audit language.		
	No		

	Master Agreement	Initials or "N/A"	Date
	Does UT have a master agreement with the supplier?		
	Yes (if yes, determine whether the master agreement covers the goods/ services; if so, use master agreement).		
	No		

	Framework Order	Initials or "N/A"	Date
	Does UT have an active framework order with the supplier?		
	Yes		
	No		

Template	Initials or "N/A"	Date
Does UT have a template with the supplier?		
Yes (if yes, use the template)		
No		

Exceptions	Initials or "N/A"	Date
Process exception memo		
Send side-letter		

Minors on Campus	Initials or "N/A"	Date
Will minors be involved? See UT policy.		
Yes (add appropriate contract language)		
No		

Advanced Payment	Initials or "N/A"	Date
Will UT be required to pay in advance?		
Yes (be sure to discuss with appropriate CBO)		
No		

Trademarks/Copyrights/Intellectual Property/Licensing	Initials or "N/A"	Date
Are trademarks, copyrights, intellectual property, or licensing involved?		
Yes (if yes, then send to [named person or title] [Licensing] and [named person or title] [Office of General Counsel] for review.		
No		

	Foreign Party?	Initials or "N/A"	Date
	Determine whether Export Control issues are involved.		
	Yes (if yes, send to [Export Control officer])		
	No		

	Exclusivity Obligations?	Initials or "N/A"	Date
	Does the agreement contain exclusivity obligations (or requirements obligations)?		
	Yes (send to [named person or title] for review)		
	No		

	Financial Services, Banking, etc.	Initials or "N/A"	Date
	Does the agreement relate to financial services, banking, ATMs, credit cards, etc.?		
	Yes (if yes, send to [named person or title])		
	No		

	Bid?	Initials or "N/A"	Date
	Was this agreement bid?		
	Yes (if yes, be sure to send a draft to the buyer for their review before you make any revisions).		
	No		
	Check with buyer if you change the term (date), scope, dollars, cancellation, etc.		

Office of General Counsel	Initials or "N/A"	Date
The Office of General Counsel has reviewed.		
Yes		
Review not required by policy, and I do not have questions for the Office of General Counsel		

UT Employee Is Other Party	Initials	Date
Is UT employee the other party?		
If Yes:		
Be sure to send to the Office of General Counsel. If Coach contract, send to [named person or title].		
Be sure to send a fully signed copy to Payroll		
No		

Substantive Terms

Wire Transfer	Initials or "N/A"	Date
If contract calls for payment to a domestic agency via wire transfer, delete the wire transfer requirement.		
Deleted		

Tax Exempt?	Initials or "N/A"	Date
I have reviewed the Controller's Office website. Is UT exempt in the state where services will be performed or goods sold?		
Yes (if yes, be sure to send a completed tax exemption certificate to the supplier before you send the contract for signature. Be sure to get the supplier to remove taxes from the costs.		
No		

	Initials or "N/A"	Date
Individual (Contract Is With)		
Is contract with an individual?		
Yes (if yes, be sure to check the UT Directory to see if the person's name appears. Also, check with director to run a search in PA20)		
No		

	Initials or "N/A"	Date
Tax Exempt Bonds		
Will a private-sector supplier be using UT space to provide goods or services?		
Yes (if yes, send to [named person or title])		
No		

	Initials or "N/A"	Date
Capital Improvements		
Does the contract involve any construction, renovation, installation, demolition or other services that relate to altering (in any way) a UT building or plot of real property?		
Yes (if service is $85,000 or more, please contact director)		
No.		
Will supplier be making capital improvements to UT property (often arises in Aramark, Sodexo, etc., agreements)		
Yes (if yes, send to [named person or title] for their guidance on the correct language to include)		
No		

European Union GDPR	Initials or "N/A"	Date
Include UT's standard GDPR language, when applicable. GDPR will often be an issue in the following contexts:		
EU campuses, affiliates, and programs Study abroad Development Alumni relations Admissions Online learning/distance education Online sales of UT merchandise Purchases of equipment for research		

Contract Macro	Initials or "N/A"	Date
I applied the contract macro, I reviewed the macro's highlights, and I made appropriate changes. You must use the macro on all Word documents, unless you are reviewing a UT template.		

Department's Obligations	Initials or "N/A"	Date
If the contract contains non-standard obligations for the department, such as verifying that a room is a certain size; that the department will delete copies of software after the license expires; etc., verify with the department via email that the department can, and will, comply.		

Deletions: Handle Deletions Correctly

Accept All Changes and Remove Comments	Initials or "N/A"	Date
After both parties have agreed to the final version, accept all changes and remove all comments.		

	Initials or "N/A"	Date
Auto Renewal		
You must delete any automatic renewal clause.		

	Initials or "N/A"	Date
Removing Clauses		
If you remove an entire clause, be sure to either remove the entire clause and its section header, or add "[Deleted]" in place of the deleted text. For example, "Governing Law: [Deleted]."		

Critical Compliance		
Accounts Payable	Initials or "N/A"	Date
How UT buys needs to be driven largely by how UT pays. Be sure to think through the accounts payable side of this transaction.		
Obtain a pro forma invoice from the vendor. Make sure that the contract's description of goods or services (or both) match what the invoice will say.		

	Initials or "N/A"	Date
Insurance		
Review risk management's insurance and bonding guidelines.		
Add appropriate insurance language, when needed.		

	Initials or "N/A"	Date
Bonds		
If the contract is for construction, remodeling, renovations, demolition or similar services, at $100,000 or more, ask Facilities Planning whether UT needs to require a payment bond.		

State Building Commission	Initials or "N/A"	Date
If the agreement is a lease valued at $25,000 or more; **or** the term is 5 years or longer, ensure that [named person or title] reviews.		
This includes a lease of parking spaces or other property.		
If the agreement relates to short-term housing for UT students, staff, faculty, or visitors, regardless of dollar value or length, ensure that [named person or title] reviews.		

Debarred Vendors	Initials or "N/A"	Date
Check the state of TN's debarred vendor list to ensure that the vendor does not appear on the list: https://www.tn.gov/generalservices/procurement/central-procurement-office—cpo-/local-units-of-governments-/procurement-information.html		
Check SAM.gov to ensure that the vendor has not been debarred by the U.S. federal government. https://www.sam.gov/portal/SAM/#1#1		

Final Steps

Signature	Initials or "N/A"	Date
I am sending the fully negotiated, mutually acceptable version for signature.		
If sending via DocuSign, I have notified the supplier that UT will sign via DocuSign. The supplier has agreed to sign via DocuSign, and I have the appropriate contact information.		
If UTSA will sign, I have reviewed the signature guidelines, and I understand where to send this contract for signature.		

	Revisions	Initials	Date
	I have made appropriate revisions under all applicable UT Policies and the Contract Manual.		
	Yes		
	No (due to an exception)		

	Redactions (black-outs)	Initials	Date
	I have removed all sensitive information from the contract via Adobe's redaction tool. Be sure to redact social security numbers, personally identifiable health information, and any other information tied to an individual person. *You do not need to redact corporation bank account or wire instructions.*		
	Yes		
	No		

	Attestation and Disclaimer	Initials	Date
	Disclaimer: By using this checklist, I understand that this checklist is for guidance purposes only. Further, I understand that I am fully responsible for complying with all appropriate policies, the Contract Manual, and other rules or guidelines. I understand that this checklist is not guaranteed to be comprehensive.		
	I attest that I agree to the disclaimer, and I attest that my responses above are accurate.		

Upload fully signed copy into contract management system, and upload a copy of this completed checklist.			
	Be sure to upload separate files as separate uploads.		

Appendix B

Model Standard Payable Contract

This standard accounts payable agreement is dated ____ and is between [your organization] ("University") and _____ ("Supplier").

The parties agree as follows:

A. Term and scope:

    1. Term: This agreement begins on the date listed in the introductory clause and ends on _____.

    2. Termination:

        i. For cause: If Supplier materially breaches this agreement, University may terminate this agreement immediately.

        ii. Unrestricted right: Either party may terminate this agreement for any reason by giving the other party at least 30 days' prior notice.

        iii. Work: If University terminates this agreement, upon receipt of University's notice of termination, Supplier shall immediately stop all work under this agreement.

    3. Scope: See Schedule 1.

B. Financial:

    1. Compensation: See Schedule 1.

    2. Invoices:

        i. Required: Supplier shall invoice the University.

        ii. Invoice contents: Supplier must include the following information on its invoices under this agreement:

1. Addressed to the University

2. Invoice number (assigned by Supplier)

3. Invoice date

4. Transaction date

5. Supplier name

6. Supplier contact for invoice questions (name, phone, or email)

7. Supplier remittance address

8. Description of delivered goods or services provided and invoiced, including identifying information as applicable

9. Number of delivered or completed units, increments, hours, or days, as applicable, of each good or service invoiced

10. Amount due for each compensable unit of good or service; and

11. Total amount due for the invoice period

iii. <u>Late payment</u>: University's payment will not be considered late unless University pays later than 45 days after receiving Supplier's invoice.

3. <u>Records; audit</u>:

i. <u>Records</u>: Supplier will maintain records for all expenses for which Supplier invoices the University under this agreement. Supplier will maintain its records for at least three years and will maintain its records in accordance with generally accepted accounting principles.

ii. <u>Audit</u>: During the term of this agreement and for three years after the last payment from the University to Supplier under this agreement, the State of Tennessee Comptroller or the University's internal audit, or both, may audit Supplier's records that relate to this agreement.

iii. <u>Assistance</u>: Supplier shall provide the University with any documentation, access to information, or other assistance necessary for the University to ensure that Supplier complies with its obligations under this agreement.

C. <u>Compliance</u>:

1. <u>Conflicts of interest</u>:

i. Supplier states that no part of the Supplier's compensation will be paid directly or indirectly to an employee or official of the State of Tennessee as wages, compensation, or gifts in exchange for acting as an officer, agent, employee, subcontractor, or consultant to the Supplier in connection with any work contemplated or performed under this Contract.

ii. Supplier states that this Contract is immediately void if the Supplier is, or within the past six months has been, an employee of the State of Tennessee or if the Supplier is an entity in which a controlling interest is held by an individual who is, or within the past six months has been, an employee of the State of Tennessee.

2. <u>Debarment</u>: Supplier hereby states that the following are true statements:

   i. Supplier is not currently debarred by the U.S. federal government.

   ii. Supplier is not currently suspended by the U.S. federal government.

   iii. Supplier is not currently named as an "excluded" supplier by the U.S. federal government.

3. <u>Background checks</u>:

   i. <u>General obligation</u>: Supplier will not knowingly assign any individual to provide services to University if the individual has a history of criminal conduct. For proposes of this agreement, "criminal conduct" means charges filed by any government agency, excluding nonmoving violations and speeding violations.

   ii. <u>Prompt background checks</u>: If the University requests, Supplier must perform a comprehensive criminal background check on any Supplier employee or subcontractor.

4. <u>Premises rules</u>: When Supplier is physically present on University property, Supplier shall make reasonable efforts to cause its employees and permitted subcontractors to become aware of, and in full compliance with, University's rules, practices, and policies (collectively referred to as "rules."). For example, Supplier shall ensure that it complies with the University's applicable rules regarding safety, smoking, noise, access restrictions, parking, security, and consideration for minors (students and University visitors under age 18).

5. <u>Conduct</u>: Supplier will make reasonable efforts to ensure that Supplier's employees and subcontractors will conduct themselves in a professional manner while on University property and while interacting with University employees, students, or visitors. Supplier must report within 24 hours to the University's Office of Procurement Services any complaints about Supplier's employees or subcontractors engaging in the following behavior: sexually suggestive or harassing behavior; unwanted physical touching; unwanted photographs; alcohol use; illegal drug use; or physical manifestations of alcohol or drug use (e.g., Supplier's employee emits smells that indicate that the individual consumed alcohol recently).

D. <u>Insurance</u>: Supplier shall comply with Schedule 2 (Insurance).

E. <u>General</u>:

1. <u>Assignment</u>: This agreement is personal to Supplier. Accordingly, Supplier may not assign any rights or delegate any duties under this agreement.

2. <u>Independent supplier</u>: The parties intend for their relationship to be that of independent contractors. Supplier acknowledges that it is not an employee of University.

3. <u>Governing law</u>: The laws of the state of Tennessee, without giving effect to its principles of conflicts of law, govern this agreement.

4. <u>Use of University intellectual property</u>: Except as allowed in this section, Supplier shall not use the University's name, logo, or any other University-owned intellectual property for any reason without the written consent of an authorized official of the University. During the term of this agreement, Supplier may list the University's name in Supplier's list of clients.

5. <u>Third-party beneficiaries</u>: There are no third-party beneficiaries to this agreement.

6. <u>Severability</u>: The parties intend as follows:

   i. That if any provision of this agreement is held to be unenforceable, that provision will be modified to the minimum extent necessary to make it enforceable, unless that modification is not permitted by law, in which case that provision will be disregarded;

   ii. That if an unenforceable provision is modified or disregarded in accordance with this section, the rest of the agreement will remain in effect as written; and

   iii. That any unenforceable provision will remain as written in any circumstances other than those in which the provision is held to be unenforceable.

7. <u>Modification; waiver</u>:

   i. <u>Modification</u>:

      1. No amendment of this agreement will be effective unless (1) it is in writing, (2) it is signed by authorized officials of both parties, and (3) it specifically references this agreement.

      2. Only the University's authorized officials have the authority to bind the University. A list of the University's authorized officials is located here: http://treasurer.tennessee.edu/contracts /contractsignature.html

   ii. <u>Waiver</u>: No waiver of satisfaction of a condition or failure to comply with an obligation under this agreement will be effective unless it is in writing and signed by the party granting the waiver, and no such waiver will constitute a waiver of satisfaction of any other condition or failure to comply with any other obligation.

8. <u>Counterparts</u>: If the parties sign this agreement in several counterparts, each will be deemed an original, but all counterparts together will constitute one instrument.

9. <u>Force majeure</u>: Neither party's delay or failure to perform any provision of this agreement as result of circumstances beyond its control (including, without limitation, war; strikes; floods; governmental restrictions; power, telecommunications, or Internet failures; or damage to or destruction of any network facilities) will be deemed a breach of this agreement.

10. <u>Notice</u>:

    i. For a notice or other communication under this agreement to be valid, it must be in writing and delivered (1) by hand, (2) by a national transportation company, with all fees prepaid, or (3) by registered or certified mail, return receipt requested and postage prepaid;

    ii. Subject to subsection (iv) below, a valid notice or other communication under this agreement will be effective when received by the party to which it is addressed. It will be deemed to have been received as follows:

        1. If it is delivered by hand, delivered by a national transportation company, with all fees prepaid, or delivered by registered or certified mail, return receipt requested and postage prepaid, upon receipt as indicated by the date on the signed receipt; and

        2. If the party to which it is addressed rejects or otherwise refuses to accept it, or if it cannot be delivered because of a change in address for which no notice was given, then upon that rejection, refusal, or inability to deliver.

    iii. For a notice or other communication to a party under this agreement to be valid, it must be addressed using the information specified below for that party or any other information specified by that party in a notice in accordance with this section.

    Supplier:

        [add]

    University:

        [add]

    iv. If a notice or other communication addressed to a party is received after 5:00 p.m. on a business day at the location specified in the address for that party or on a day that is not a business day, the notice will be deemed received at 9:00 a.m. on the next business day.

F. <u>Entire agreement</u>: This agreement constitutes the entire understanding between the parties with respect to the subject matter of this agreement and supersedes all other agreements, whether written or oral, between the parties. In the event that Supplier maintains terms and conditions on its website, software, invoices, and so on, such terms and conditions do not apply to the University.

The parties are signing this agreement on the date listed in the introductory clause.

Supplier	**[your organization]**
Signature: _____	Signature: _____
Name: _____	Name: _____
Title: _____	Title: _____

Schedule 1: Scope and Financial

1. <u>Scope</u>:

2. <u>Compensation</u>:

3. <u>Travel</u>:

[add details, as needed]

Appendix C

Sample Visitor Hotel Rate Agreement

This hotel agreement is dated _____ and is between _____
("University"), and _____ ("Hotel").

Background:

a) University has many prospective students who visit the University each year.

b) To help visiting students and their families, the University wants to obtain discounted rates and other benefits for the visiting students and their families.

c) Hotel has lodging facilities located in the _____ area.

d) Hotel and University enter into this agreement with the intent of providing discounts to the University's visiting prospective students.

e) This agreement is not for the University's use. Accordingly, University departments may not use this agreement to spend University funds or conduct any University business.

Agreement: The parties agree as follows:

1) **Scope:**

    a. <u>Purpose</u>: In support of its education mission, the University enters into this agreement with Hotel to offer discounted hotel sleeping room rates to potential students, their families, and similar visitors to The University of Tennessee's Knoxville-area departments (includes visiting students for the University's Knoxville Campus, Institute of Agriculture, and the Institute for Public Service).

    b. <u>No third-party beneficiaries</u>: There are no third-party beneficiaries to this agreement.

c. <u>No obligation</u>: The parties acknowledge that the University incurs no obligations under this agreement, except to make reasonable efforts to advertise the existence of this agreement. For clarity, this agreement does not impose any financial obligation on the University. *The University's departments cannot use this agreement for official University business or to spend University funds.*

2) **Term and Termination:**

a. <u>Initial term</u>: The initial term of this agreement begins on the date listed in the introductory clause and ends at 11:59 p.m. Eastern Time on December 31, _____.

b. <u>Renewal term</u>: Upon mutual written agreement, the parties may extend this agreement on an annual basis (the first renewal would start on January 1, ____).

c. <u>Auto renewal prohibited</u>: This agreement does not automatically renew.

d. <u>Unrestricted termination</u>: The University may terminate this agreement for any reason, or no reason, by providing the Hotel with at least 10 days' prior notice. Upon receiving notice, the Hotel shall stop all work.

3) **Recommended Hotel Designation:** The University will refer to Hotel as a "recommended" Hotel. The University will not refer to Hotel as "preferred." University will post Hotel's information and a link to Hotel's booking website on the University's website located at [add link].

4) **Rates and Blackout Dates:** See Schedule A.

5) **Rate Code(s):** See Schedule A.

6) **Additional Offerings:** See Schedule A.

7) **University Materials:** Hotel will make reasonable efforts to participate in events and promotions through the University's Office of Admissions, including distributing University materials.

8) **Information:** Hotel will make reasonable efforts to distribute University-provided literature, maps, and so on to individuals using the Hotel's rate codes under this agreement. University acknowledges that guests must use the rate codes provided under this agreement before Hotel will distribute items to guests.

9) **Not Exclusive:** This agreement is not exclusive.

10) **General**

a. **Modification; Wavier:**

i. <u>Modification</u>: No amendment of this agreement will be effective unless it is in writing and signed by authorized officials of both parties. Only the University's authorized officials have the authority to bind the University. A list of the University's authorized officials is located here: [add link].

ii. <u>Waiver</u>: No waiver of satisfaction of a condition or failure to comply with an obligation under this agreement will be effective unless it is in writing and signed by the party granting the waiver, and no such waiver will constitute a waiver of satisfaction of any other condition or failure to comply with any other obligation.

b. **Force Majeure**: Neither party's delay or failure to perform any provision of this agreement as result of circumstances beyond its control (including, without limitation, war; strikes; floods; governmental restrictions; power, telecommunications, or Internet failures; or damage to or destruction of any network facilities) will be deemed a breach of this agreement.

c. **Dispute Resolution**: The parties shall make reasonable efforts to resolve any dispute before filing any formal legal action. Accordingly, the parties shall make good-faith efforts to resolve any disputes amicably.

d. **Assignment**: This agreement is personal to the University, and the University may not assign its rights or delegate its duties under this agreement.

e. **Waiver of Claims**:

i. <u>Respondent's intent</u>: Hotel intends to protect the University's employees from personal liability. Accordingly, Hotel intends to waive and release any claims against the University's employees.

ii. <u>Irrevocable waiver</u>: Hotel hereby irrevocably waives any claims against the University's employees or former employees. Hotel hereby covenants not to sue University employees or former employees in their individual capacity. This release and waiver applies to Hotel and Hotel's successors, heirs, and assigns.

iii. <u>Materiality</u>: The University and Hotel state that this clause is material to this agreement.

f. **Use of University Intellectual Property**: Except as allowed in this section, Hotel shall not use the University's name, logo, or any other University-owned intellectual property for any reason without the written consent of an authorized official of the University. During the term of this agreement, Hotel may list the University's name in Hotel's list of clients.

g. **Third-Party Beneficiaries**: There are no third-party beneficiaries to this agreement.

h. **Severability**: The parties intend as follows:

i. That if any provision of this agreement is held to be unenforceable, that provision will be modified to the minimum extent necessary to make it enforceable, unless that modification is not permitted by law, in which case that provision will be disregarded

ii. That if an unenforceable provision is modified or disregarded in accordance with this section, then the rest of the agreement will remain in effect as written

iii. That any unenforceable provision will remain as written in any circumstances other than those in which the provision is held to be unenforceable

11) **Notice:**

a. For a notice or other communication under this agreement to be valid, it must be in writing and delivered (1) by hand, (2) by a national transportation company, with all fees prepaid, or (3) by registered or certified mail, return receipt requested and postage prepaid.

b. Subject to subsection (d) below, a valid notice or other communication under this agreement will be effective when received by the party to which it is addressed. It will be deemed to have been received as follows:

   i. If it is delivered by hand, delivered by a national transportation company, with all fees prepaid, or delivered by registered or certified mail, return receipt requested and postage prepaid, upon receipt as indicated by the date on the signed receipt

   ii. If the party to which it is addressed rejects or otherwise refuses to accept it, or if it cannot be delivered because of a change in address for which no notice was given, then upon that rejection, refusal, or inability to deliver

c. For a notice or other communication to a party under this agreement to be valid, it must be addressed using the information specified below for that party or any other information specified by that party in a notice in accordance with this section.

   Hotel:

   See Schedule A.

   University:

   [add]

d. If a notice or other communication addressed to a party is received after 5:00 p.m. on a business day at the location specified in the address for that party or on a day that is not a business day, then the notice will be deemed received at 9:00 a.m. on the next business day.

12) **Entire Agreement:** This agreement constitutes the entire understanding between the parties with respect to the subject matter of this agreement and supersedes all other agreements, whether written or oral, between the parties. In the event Hotel's website, mobile applications, or other platforms containing click-wrap, browse-wrap, or shrink-wrap terms and conditions, Hotel states that such terms and conditions do not apply to University.

Agreed: The parties are signing this agreement on the date listed in the introductory clause.

Hotel	**[your organization]**
Signature: _____	Signature: _____
Name: _____	Name: _____
Title: _____	Title: _____

Schedule A

Hotel's Address for Notices:

Rate:

Rate Code:

Blackout Dates:

Additional Offerings:

Appendix D

Sample Preferred Hotel Agreement

This hotel services master agreement is dated _____ and is between [your organization] ("University") and _____ ("Hotel").

Agreement: The parties agree as follows:

1) **Purpose and Scope**: This agreement will govern all transactions between University and Hotel during the term of this agreement. This agreement is available to all of the University's departments at any University campus. This agreement applies to the following situations:

   a. When the University pays the Hotel directly (commonly referred to as "direct bill")

   b. When a University employee or University guest traveler books a sleeping room while on official University business

   c. When the University organizes a University-sponsored event, and attendees (includes individuals who are not University employees) pay their own sleeping room costs

2) **Preferred Hotel**: University hereby designates the Hotel as one of the University's "preferred hotels."

3) **Term and Termination**:

   a. Term of master agreement: This agreement is effective at 12:01 a.m. Eastern Time on the date listed in the introductory clause and ends at 11:59 p.m. Eastern Time on _____. In addition to governing transactions that are booked and occur during the term of this agreement, this agreement governs any transactions booked during the term of this agreement but which actually occur after this agreement expires or is terminated in accordance with (3)d.

b. Term of individual room stay: Individuals will book their rooms, and the length of the stay will be reflected in the Hotel's booking system.

c. Term of each group event: The term of any group event (e.g., meetings, group room blocks, etc.) will be stated in mutually agreed Event Order Forms. All Event Order Forms are governed by the terms of this agreement, and any terms and conditions listed in the Event Order Forms do not apply. University's departments may sign banquet event orders (BEOs).

d. Termination of this master agreement: Either party may terminate this agreement by providing the other party with 60 days' prior written notice.

4) **Financial**:

a. Advanced payments: Hotel will not require University to make any advance payments, including deposits.

b. Sleeping rooms:

i. Blackout dates: The parties will update Schedule 1 each calendar year to reflect blackout dates.

ii. CONUS rates: For all of Hotel's standard rooms, Hotel will offer CONUS rates for Knoxville, as listed by the U.S. federal government's General Services Administration. Hotel's standard room inventory consists of [list the standard rooms]. This rate applies to rooms booked as part of a group and for individual travelers.

iii. Lowest rate guarantee: Hotel agrees to honor lower rates that may exist during any of the meeting dates. Rates offered under contract to wholesalers are exempt from this requirement.

iv. Last-room availability: Hotel will offer CONUS rates on a "last room availability" basis every day (i.e., the Hotel will offer the University CONUS rates on all available rooms, including the last room available on any given night). In other words, if the Hotel has one standard room left, Hotel will offer CONUS rates to the University.

v. Oversold/"walk" procedures: If Hotel oversells its rooms and a room is not available for a University guest holding a reservation, Hotel will:

1. Pay for a room at a comparable hotel for each night the guest is displaced (i.e., each night Hotel cannot provide the guest a room).

2. Provide transportation to the comparable hotel. If the guest is attending a group event at Hotel, then Hotel will provide transportation to and from the Hotel each day that the guest is displaced.

3. Provide one long-distance telephone call and access to the Internet while guest awaits transportation to the comparable hotel.

4. Provide the guest a room at Hotel as soon as possible.

vi. <u>Check-in/check-out</u>:

    1. <u>Check-in</u>: The Hotel's check-in time is 3 p.m. Eastern Time. Upon guest request, Hotel will make reasonable efforts to offer an early check-in at no extra charge.

    2. <u>Check-out</u>: The Hotel's check-out time is 12:00 p.m. Eastern Time. Upon guest request, Hotel will make a reasonable effort to offer a late check-out at no extra charge, not to exceed 1:30 p.m. Easter Time.

vii. <u>Early departure fees</u>: Hotel will waive a guest's early departure fees.

viii. <u>Cancellation</u>: Individuals may cancel their reservation without penalty by cancelling no later than 11:59 p.m. Eastern Time the day before arrival.

c. <u>Events:</u>

    i. <u>Generally</u>: Beginning no less than 3 months from the start of an event, Hotel will provide a University department who has booked an event with weekly updates regarding the number of rooms booked, number of rooms remaining in group room block, and potential attrition damages. Hotel will also provide information on meeting space and discuss possible adjustments, as needed.

    ii. <u>Assistance</u>: Hotel shall advise each University department on calculating the appropriate group size and room block. Before the University signs the first BEO for a particular event (i.e., before the University is contractually obligated for the event), Hotel must ensure that the University department seeking to book the event understands the consequences for attrition and cancellation.

    iii. <u>Event cancellation</u>:

        1. [insert matrix of cancellation]

        2. On each BEO, Hotel must clearly state possible attrition and cancellation charges, if applicable.

    iv. <u>Group room block (GRB)</u>:

        1. Hotel will not sell any rooms in the group room block until after the cut-ff date without obtaining the University's written consent. Hotel will continue to honor the group rate after the cutoff date as long as any rooms remain available.

        2. Hotel will allow the group room block to be exceeded by a minimum of 10% at the agreed-upon rate as long as any rooms remain available for sale by the Hotel.

        3. Hotel will provide each group with a personalized reservation code for group attendees to make their reservations online.

4. If the Hotel sells more than 10% of the GRB, causing rooms not to be available for the University's event, the hotel will pay the University an amount equal to 25% of the rate for each room in the GRB not available for booking by the University.

5. For each GRB, Hotel will provide 1 free guest room for every 35 booked.

6. For each GRB exceeding 35 rooms, Hotel will provide one VIP suite on a complimentary basis and will attempt to accommodate complimentary upgrades for VIPs.

7. Hotel agrees to allow room substitutions at the group rate up to the date of the event.

v. Room block attrition:

1. The University may change event details, including the size of the room block, up to 21 days before arrival without penalties or fees.

2. The University will be responsible for a portion of nights not utilized on a cumulative basis below 80% of the total group room block after the cutoff date (21 days prior to the event).

3. The parties agree that the University will pay attrition as follows: 75% of the negotiated room rate × (rooms not used under 80%). When paying an attrition fee, the University will not pay for service charges or taxes. Hotel will review the proposed attrition damages with the University's Procurement Services Office before charging the University.

4. Hotel will credit University's group room block for all reservations made and used by the University meeting attendees, regardless of the rate paid or method of booking, including all reservations made after the cutoff date.

vi. If Hotel achieves occupancy levels of at least 90% of total available rooms (excluding oversell) during any night of a University event, the University will not be required to pay attrition damages.

d. Food and beverage:

i. The University's food and beverage needs will be stated in BEOs.

ii. University will provide Hotel with a final head-count no later than 72 hours before the event. University may adjust its food order up to 72 hours before the event without penalties or costs.

e. Meeting rooms:

i. University will book meeting space via BEOs.

ii. University may alter or cancel its meeting space without penalties no less than 21 days in advance of the event.

   iii. Hotel will provide, at no additional cost to the University, sufficient quantities of standard meeting and banquet supplies, such as tables, chairs, platforms, risers, lecterns, utensils, etc.

   iv. Hotel will provide one complimentary easel for signage at each meeting room doorway, if requested.

   v. Hotel will not release the University's meeting space without first obtaining the University's written approval.

 f. Audiovisual:

   i. The University may bring its own audiovisual equipment at no additional cost.

   ii. The University may contract with a third party to provide audiovisual goods and services at no extra cost to University. The University will not agree to be responsible for the acts and omissions of third parties.

 g. Taxes: When the University pays costs directly, the Hotel will not charge the University taxes.

 h. Internet: Hotel will provide Internet access to guests' sleeping rooms and to meeting attendees at no charge.

 i. Service charge: Hotel may charge a 20% service charge for meeting space, audiovisual equipment provided by the Hotel, and group food and beverage.

 j. Parking: [add]

 k. Invoicing and payment: [add]

   i. Groups:

   ii. Individual direct billed rooms:

   iii. Payment: University will pay Hotel via ACH transfer within 30 days after receiving Hotel's invoice.

5) **Data Reporting**: [add]

6) **Obligation to Mitigate Damages**: Hotel shall make reasonable efforts to resell unused University rooms, meeting space, etc., in an effort to reduce any liquidated damages.

7) **Noninterference and Quality**:

 a. Quiet enjoyment: Hotel states that Hotel will ensure University's ordinary use and quiet enjoyment of Hotel.

 b. Incompatible events: [add]

 c. Construction: [add]

8) **Force Majeure**: The University will not be responsible for any costs, including attrition or cancellation fees, if the University (including an individual)

cancels due to a force majeure occurrence (any event that is beyond the University's reasonable control that makes conducting the event impractical or impossible).

9) **General Terms:**

a. Americans with Disabilities Act (ADA): Hotel states that it will maintain compliance with the ADA.

b. Assignment: This agreement is personal to the parties. Neither party may assign any of their rights or delegate any of their obligations under this agreement to any other person or entity. In the event that Hotel's management company changes during the term of this agreement, Hotel must notify University as soon as possible. University may terminate any BEO without liability.

c. Audit: The Hotel shall maintain records for all charges against the University under this agreement. Hotel shall maintain its records for three full years after receiving final payment from the University. Hotel shall maintain its records in accordance with generally accepted accounting principles. During the term of this agreement and for 3 years after the University delivers final payment to the Hotel, the University or the Comptroller of the State of Tennessee, or both, may audit Hotel's records related to this agreement.

d. Compliance with laws: Both parties will comply with applicable laws and regulations.

e. Governing law: The internal laws of the State of Tennessee, without giving effect to its principles of conflicts of law, govern this agreement. The University's liability is governed by the Tennessee Claims Commission Act.

f. Illegal immigrants: In compliance with the requirements of Tenn. Code Ann. § 12-3-309, Hotel hereby attests that it shall not knowingly utilize the services of an illegal immigrant in the United States in the performance of this agreement and shall not knowingly utilize the services of any subcontractor who will utilize the services of an illegal immigrant in the United States in the performance of this agreement.

g. Modification; wavier: No amendment of this agreement will be effective unless it is in writing and signed by the parties. No waiver of satisfaction of a condition or failure to comply with an obligation under this agreement will be effective unless it is in writing and signed by the party granting the waiver, and no such waiver will constitute a waiver of satisfaction of any other condition or failure to comply with any other obligation.

h. No obligation on University to make purchases/not exclusive: The parties agree that this master agreement does not obligate University to make any purchases from Hotel. Further, this agreement does not create an exclusive arrangement between University and Hotel. For the sake of clarity, binding commitments will be made on an event-by-event/ booking-by-booking basis via room reservations or Hotel's BEO forms.

i. Sales tax registration: In compliance with the requirements of Tenn. Code Ann. § 12-3-306, the Hotel hereby attests that it has registered with the State of Tennessee's Department of Revenue for the collection of Tennessee sales and use tax. This registration requirement is a material requirement of this agreement.

10) **Notice:**

a. For a notice or other communication under this agreement to be valid, it must be in writing and delivered (1) by hand, (2) by a national transportation company, with all fees prepaid, (3) by registered or certified mail, return receipt requested and postage prepaid, or (4) by email to the addresses listed in 10(c).

b. Subject to subsection (d) below, a valid notice or other communication under this agreement will be effective when received by the party to which it is addressed. It will be deemed to have been received as follows:

i. If it is delivered by hand, delivered by a national transportation company, with all fees prepaid, or delivered by registered or certified mail, return receipt requested and postage prepaid, upon receipt as indicated by the date on the signed receipt; and

ii. If the party to which it is addressed rejects or otherwise refuses to accept it, or if it cannot be delivered because of a change in address for which no notice was given, then upon that rejection, refusal, or inability to deliver.

c. For a notice or other communication to a party under this agreement to be valid, it must be addressed using the information specified below for that party or any other information specified by that party in a notice in accordance with this section.

Hotel:

[add]

University:

[add]

d. If a notice or other communication addressed to a party is received after 5:00 p.m. on a business day at the location specified in the address for that party or on a day that is not a business day, then the notice will be deemed received at 9:00 a.m. on the next business day

11) Severability: The parties intend as follows:

a. That if any provision of this agreement is held to be unenforceable, that provision will be modified to the minimum extent necessary to make it enforceable, unless that modification is not permitted by law, in which case that provision will be disregarded;

b. If an unenforceable provision is modified or disregarded in accordance with this section, the rest of the agreement will remain in effect as written; and

c. That any unenforceable provision will remain as written in any circumstances other than those in which the provision is held to be unenforceable.

12) Entire agreement: This agreement constitutes the entire understanding between the parties with respect to the subject matter of this agreement and supersedes all other agreements, whether written or oral, between the parties. In the event Hotel's website, mobile applications, or other platforms containing click-wrap, browse-wrap, or shrink-wrap terms and conditions, Hotel states that such terms and conditions do not apply to University.

Agreed: The parties are signing this agreement on the date listed in the introductory clause.

Hotel	**[your organization]**
Signature: _____	Signature: _____
Name: _____	Name: _____
Title: _____	Title: _____

Schedule 1

Blackout dates for _____[year]:

Appendix E

Sample Master Lease for Students

This master lease agreement is dated _____ and is between _____, a/an _____ ("Lessor"), and _____ ("University").

Background:

- The University needs to place a number of students in apartments owned by third parties.

- Lessor has space available in its apartment complex located at _____, commonly known as _____, ("complex") and has agreed to lease certain space to the University.

- The nature of the transaction between the University and Lessor is that the University will be responsible for paying rent to Lessor. Lessor will provide all deliverables described in Schedule A.

- University's students ("students") will occupy the space described in Schedule B.

- Lessor will require the students to sign agreements that bind the Lessor and students with respect to the use and occupancy of the spaces in the complex. Those agreements will relate to Lessor's rules and regulations. The University will not be a party to those agreements and, accordingly, is not bound by those agreements.

Agreement: Lessor and University agree as follows:

1. **Term**: The term of this agreement begins at 12:01 a.m. Eastern Time on _____ and ends at 11:59 p.m. Eastern Time on _____.

2. **Termination**:

   a. **When allowed:**

      i. **By lessor**: Except as permitted under the Uniform Residential Landlord Tenant Act, Lessor may only terminate this agreement for any specific unit if the student materially violates Lessor's rules and regulations and after providing not less than five days' written notice to the University.

ii. <u>By university</u>: Upon not less than 30 days' notice, University may terminate this agreement for any specific unit if:

1. A student occupying a unit withdraws from enrollment at the University

2. University housing space becomes available

iii. <u>Automatic</u>: This agreement will automatically terminate for any particular unit if the student occupying that unit dies.

b. <u>Notice requirement</u>: Either party must provide termination notice to the other in accordance with the Notice section of this agreement.

c. <u>Effect</u>: In the event that either party terminates this agreement for any particular unit, the University's obligation to pay for the unit will end on the effective date of the notice.

3. **<u>Deliverables and Lease</u>:**

a. <u>Deliverables</u>: Lessor will provide the deliverables stated in Schedule A for as long as a unit is subject to this agreement. Lessor shall not charge the students for anything stated in Schedule A.

b. <u>Lease</u>: Lessor hereby leases to University and University hereby leases from Lessor the property ("units") described in Schedule B, together with rights to utilize all common areas associated with the apartment complex in which the units are located.

4. **<u>Payment</u>:** University shall pay the amounts listed in Schedule A. University shall pay Lessor the first installment by _____, and each monthly installment thereafter by the 1st day of each month via ACH transfer. In the event that the University fails to pay by the 6th of each month, Lessor may charge a 1.5% late payment fee. Payment in full of the amounts set forth in Schedule A will constitute payment by University for the units and all services provided by Lessor under this agreement; neither University nor the students will be responsible for any charges for taxes, insurance, utilities, maintenance, or any other items, except for costs associated with repairs to damages caused by students, which will be the obligation of the student(s) causing such damage.

5. **<u>Condition of Premises</u>:** Lessor shall deliver possession of the units beginning at _____ Eastern Time on the date listed in Section 1. Lessor states that the units are in good order and repair.

6. **<u>Damages</u>:**

a. <u>Generally</u>: ***The University is not responsible for the acts or omissions of its students.*** The University's sole obligation under this agreement is to pay the rent amounts listed in Schedule A. Accordingly, Lessor acknowledges that the individual residents are responsible for any costs associated with damages.

b. <u>Ordinary wear and tear</u>: Students will not be liable for ordinary wear and tear.

7. **Rules and Regulations**: The University is not responsible for the students' compliance with Lessor's rules and regulations. Lessor is responsible for ensuring that students are aware of Lessor's rules and regulations.

8. **Maintenance and Repairs**: Lessor shall maintain the units and the complex in good working order and in the same condition or better as exists on the date of this agreement. Lessor will ensure that the students are aware of how to request maintenance, including repairs.

9. **Fire and Other Casualties**: In the case of damage by fire or other casualty to the building in which the units are located, if the damage is so extensive as to render the units untenable, this agreement will terminate immediately for the affected units, and the rental costs will be apportioned to the time of the fire or casualty.

10. **Records; Audit**:

a. <u>Records</u>: Lessor will maintain records for all expenses for which Lessor invoices the University under this agreement. Lessor will maintain its records for at least 5 years and will maintain its records in accordance with generally accepted accounting principles.

b. <u>Audit</u>: During the term of this agreement and for 5 years after the last payment from the University to Lessor under this agreement, University's internal audit may audit Lessor's records that relate to this agreement.

11. **Debarment**: Lessor hereby states that the following are true statements:

a. Lessor is not currently debarred by the U.S. federal government.

b. Lessor is not currently suspended by the U.S. federal government.

c. Lessor is not currently named as an "excluded" Lessor by the U.S. federal government.

12. **Background Checks**:

a. <u>General obligation</u>: Lessor will not knowingly assign any individual to provide services to University if the individual has a history of criminal conduct. For purposes of this agreement, "criminal conduct" means charges filed by any government agency, excluding nonmoving violations and speeding violations.

b. <u>Prompt background checks</u>: If the University requests, Lessor must perform a comprehensive criminal background check on any Lessor employee or subcontractor.

13. **Reporting**: If Lessor has actual knowledge of the items below, Lessor shall notify the University immediately if any of the following items occur in one

of the units or elsewhere on Lessor's premises, provided Lessor is permitted to do so by applicable law:

a. Crimes, including attempted crimes

b. Emergencies involving personal injury to a student

c. Alcohol consumption by minor students

d. Use of illegal drugs by students

14. <u>Insurance</u>: Lessor shall comply with the insurance requirements stated in Schedule C.

15. <u>Force Majeure</u>: Neither party's delay or failure to perform any provision of this agreement, as result of circumstances beyond its control (including, without limitation, war; strikes; floods; governmental restrictions; power, telecommunications, or Internet failures; or damage to or destruction of any network facilities) will be deemed a breach of this agreement.

16. <u>Dispute Resolution</u>: The parties shall make reasonable efforts to resolve any dispute before filing any formal legal action.

17. <u>Governing Law</u>: The internal laws of the state of _____, without giving effect to its principles of conflicts of law, govern this agreement.

18. <u>Notice</u>:

a. For a notice or other communication under this agreement to be valid, it must be in writing and delivered (1) by hand; (2) by a national transportation company, with all fees prepaid; or (3) by registered or certified mail, return receipt requested and postage prepaid;

b. Subject to subsection (d) below, a valid notice or other communication under this agreement will be effective when received by the party to which it is addressed. It will be deemed to have been received as follows:

i. If it is delivered by hand, delivered by a national transportation company, with all fees prepaid, or delivered by registered or certified mail, return receipt requested and postage prepaid, upon receipt as indicated by the date on the signed receipt; and

ii. If the party to which it is addressed rejects or otherwise refuses to accept it, or if it cannot be delivered because of a change in address for which no notice was given, then upon that rejection, refusal, or inability to deliver.

c. For a notice or other communication to a party under this agreement to be valid, it must be addressed using the information specified below for that party or any other information specified by that party in a notice in accordance with this section.

Lessor:

[add address here]

University:

[add address here]

d. If a notice or other communication addressed to a party is received after 5:00 p.m. on a business day at the location specified in the address for that party or on a day that is not a business day, then the notice will be deemed received at 9:00 a.m. on the next business day.

19. **Use of University Intellectual Property**: Except as allowed in this section, Lessor shall not use the University's name, logo, or any other University-owned intellectual property for any reason without the written consent of an authorized official of the University. During the term of this agreement, Lessor may list the University's name in Lessor's list of clients.

20. **Third-Party Beneficiaries**: There are no third-party beneficiaries to this agreement. The University is not party to, and is not responsible for, any agreements between the Lessor and students directly.

21. **Severability**: The parties intend as follows:

a. That if any provision of this agreement is held to be unenforceable, that provision will be modified to the minimum extent necessary to make it enforceable, unless that modification is not permitted by law, in which case that provision will be disregarded;

b. That if an unenforceable provision is modified or disregarded in accordance with this section, the rest of the agreement will remain in effect as written; and

c. That any unenforceable provision will remain as written in any circumstances other than those in which the provision is held to be unenforceable.

22. **Modification; Waiver**:

a. Modification:

i. No amendment of this agreement will be effective unless (1) it is in writing; (2) it is signed by authorized officials of both parties; and (3) it specifically references this agreement.

ii. Only the University's authorized officials have the authority to bind the University.

b. Waiver: No waiver of satisfaction of a condition or failure to comply with an obligation under this agreement will be effective unless it is in writing and signed by the party granting the waiver, and no such waiver will constitute a waiver of satisfaction of any other condition or failure to comply with any other obligation.

23. **Counterparts**: If the parties sign this agreement in several counterparts, each will be deemed an original, but all counterparts together will constitute one instrument.

24. **Compliance with Law**: Lessor shall comply with all applicable laws, including the [reference state-specific laws regarding residential leases], and the Americans with Disabilities Act.

25. **Entire Agreement**: This agreement constitutes the entire understanding between the parties with respect to the subject matter of this agreement and supersedes all other agreements, whether written or oral, between the parties. In the event Lessor's invoices, order forms, or other Lessor-provided items contain terms, Lessor acknowledges that Lessor's terms do not apply to the University. Further, in the event Lessor's website, mobile applications, or other platforms contain click-wrap, browse-wrap, or shrink-wrap terms and conditions, Lessor states that such terms and conditions do not apply to University.

26. **End of Term**: Upon termination or expiration of this agreement, the University will peaceably surrender to the Lessor the units in as good order and condition as when received, reasonable use and wear thereof and damage by earthquake, fire, public calamity, the elements, acts of God, or circumstances over which the University has no control or for which Lessor is responsible pursuant to this lease, excepted. The University will have no duty to remove any improvements or fixtures placed by it in the units or to restore any portion of the units altered by it, save and except in the event the University elects to remove any such improvement or fixture and such removal causes damages or injury to the units and then only to the extent of any such damages or injury.

The parties are signing this agreement on the date stated in the introductory clause. This agreement is not binding until signed by all parties below.

Lessee   **Lessor**

Signature: _____   Signature: _____

Name: _____   Name: _____

Title: _____   Title: _____

Schedule A

<u>Deliverables</u>:

1. <u>Electricity, HVAC, sewer and water</u>: The rental amounts listed below include the costs of all utilities (electricity, water, and sewer), which will be provided in sufficient capacities for use of the units as residential apartments.

2. <u>Wireless Internet</u>: The rental amount also includes access to wireless Internet.

3. <u>Cable television</u>: The rental amount also includes access to cable television.

4. <u>Parking</u>: Lessor will provide each unit (bedroom) with access to 1 spot per person. Lessor will waive any costs for parking and agrees to maintain its current parking-to-units ratio.

<u>Residential apartment space</u>: Space described in Schedule B.

Total number of bedrooms units leased: _____.
Total, aggregate cost: $_____.

<u>Payments</u>:

Month #	Period Start	Period End	Aggregate Amount
1	August 1, 2025	August 31, 2025	$X

Schedule B

Apartment #	Bedrooms	Rate

Schedule C

[describe insurance requirements]

Appendix F

Sample Standard Amendment

This amendment dated _____ amends the [title of original agreement] between _____ (name of one party) and _____ (name of the second party) dated [date of original agreement] ("agreement"). Except as amended below, all other terms remain unchanged.

The parties hereby amend the agreement as follows:

The parties are signing this amendment on the effective date mentioned in the introductory clause.

Signature: _____   Signature: _____

Name: _____   Name: _____

Title: _____   Title: _____

Appendix G

Sample Professional Service Contract

Licensed Massage Therapist for Athletics Department

This licensed massage therapy services agreement is dated _____ and is between [your organization] ("University") and _____, an individual independent contractor ("Contractor").

The parties agree as follows:

1. <u>Term</u>: This agreement begins at 12:01 a.m. Eastern Time on August 1, 2018, and ends at 11:59 p.m. on _____.

2. <u>Termination</u>: Either party may terminate this agreement for any reason by giving the other party at least 30 days' prior notice.

3. <u>Services</u>:

   a. <u>Massage services</u>: Contractor will provide therapeutic massage services to the University's athletes. For purposes of this agreement, "therapeutic massage" means only rubbing or kneading the recipient's body and does not include stretching, dry needling, acupuncture, instrument-assisted soft tissue manipulation, or meditation. Contractor may only use hypoallergenic, nonmedicated massage lotion.

   b. <u>Items</u>: When Contractor performs services on University property, University will provide sheets, towels, and massage tables.

   c. <u>Appointments</u>: University will be responsible for scheduling all appointments with Contractor.

   d. <u>Communication</u>: Contractor and University will communicate about the status of each athlete for which Contractor provides a massage.

   e. <u>Location</u>: Excluding travel as allowed by this agreement, Contractor must provide massage therapy services at the University's facilities.

    f. <u>Observation</u>:

      i. <u>Non-University location</u>: If University is unable to provide a University-owned facility, Contractor acknowledges that University will require a University employee or intern to be present during all massages.

      ii. <u>University location</u>: University retains discretion to require a University employee or intern to be present during massages at University-owned locations.

    g. <u>Licensure</u>: During the term of this agreement, Contractor shall maintain an active massage therapy license through the state of Tennessee's Department of Health's Board of Massage Licensure. Within five business days after signing this agreement, Contractor must provide the University with proof of Contractor's active license.

    h. <u>License status change</u>: During the term of this agreement, if Contractor's license status changes to any status other than "active," Contractor must notify the University within two business days of Contractor learning of Contractor's license status change.

    i. <u>Confidentiality</u>:

      i. <u>Generally</u>: Contractor acknowledges that Contractor will have access to confidential information, including medical/health and student information. Contractor must comply with all applicable laws, including HIPAA and FERPA. Contractor shall treat the names of all patients as confidential information.

      ii. <u>Disclosure</u>: Unless required by law, Contractor shall not disclose any confidential information to anyone, except to University staff athletic trainers or University medical personnel.

      iii. <u>Property</u>: University owns all rights to student-athlete medical records.

4. <u>Nature of relationship</u>:

    a. <u>Independent contractor</u>: The parties intend for Contractor to be an independent contractor and not a University employee. Accordingly, Contractor will be responsible for all applicable taxes, license fees, and so on. Contractor acknowledges that Contractor will not receive any insurance or other benefits from the University.

    b. <u>Not exclusive</u>: This agreement is not exclusive (i.e., the University will contract with multiple licensed massage therapists).

5. <u>Assignment</u>: This agreement is personal to Contractor. Contractor shall not transfer to any other person or entity any obligation or rights under this agreement.

6. <u>Financial</u>:

    a. <u>Hourly rate</u>: University will pay Contractor $55 per hour. Contractor may bill University for time spent on University property from the point

Contractor is ready to perform services to the point that Contractor completes the last massage for the day.

b. Invoices: Contractor will invoice the University. Contractor's invoice must bill University using the attached invoice template (see Exhibit 1).

c. Travel:

    i. Generally: University's sports teams often perform in locations other than Knoxville, Tennessee. Sometimes, University will need to invite licensed massage therapists to travel with the applicable team.

    ii. Transportation and accommodations: If Contractor travels with University, Contractor must travel using the University's transportation. University will provide Contractor with hotel accommodations.

    iii. Pay while traveling: When Contractor travels with the University, University will pay Contractor the following:

        1. Daily base rate: University will pay Contractor $50.00 per day (including the first day of travel and the last day of travel).

        2. Massage days: If Contractor provides massage services while for University when located outside of Knoxville, Tennessee, University will pay Contractor the following pay per each day that Contractor provides massage therapy services (University will pay the rates below instead of Contractor's hourly rate):

            a. Track/Cross Country/Swimming/Diving/Football: $300.00 per day; or

            b. All other sports: $250.00 per day.

    iv. No reimbursement: University will not reimburse Contractor for any costs that Contractor incurs while traveling with the University.

7. Records; audit:

a. Records: Contractor will maintain records for all expenses for which Contractor invoices the University under this agreement. Contractor will maintain its records for at least 3 years and will maintain its records in accordance with generally accepted accounting principles.

b. Audit: During the term of this agreement and for 3 years after the last payment from the University to Contractor under this agreement, the state of Tennessee Comptroller or the University's internal audit, or both, may audit Contractor's records that relate to this agreement.

8. Force majeure: Neither party's delay or failure to perform any provision of this agreement as result of circumstances beyond its control (including, without limitation, war; strikes; floods; governmental restrictions; power, telecommunications, or Internet failures; or damage to or destruction of any network facilities) will be deemed a breach of this agreement.

9. Dispute resolution: The parties shall make reasonable efforts to resolve any dispute before filing any formal legal action.

10. Governing law: The internal laws of the state of Tennessee, without giving effect to its principles of conflicts of law, govern this agreement. The University's liability is governed by the Tennessee Claims Commission Act.

11. Severability: The parties intend as follows:

   a. That if any provision of this agreement is held to be unenforceable, that provision will be modified to the minimum extent necessary to make it enforceable, unless that modification is not permitted by law, in which case that provision will be disregarded;

   b. That if an unenforceable provision is modified or disregarded in accordance with this section, the rest of the agreement will remain in effect as written; and

   c. That any unenforceable provision will remain as written in any circumstances other than those in which the provision is held to be unenforceable.

12. Modification; waiver:

   a. Modification:

      i. No amendment of this agreement will be effective unless (1) it is in writing; (2) it is signed by authorized officials of both parties; and (3) it specifically references this agreement.

      ii. Only the University's authorized officials have the authority to bind the University. A list of the University's authorized officials is located here: http://treasurer.tennessee.edu/contracts/contractsignature.html

   b. Waiver: No waiver of satisfaction of a condition or failure to comply with an obligation under this agreement will be effective unless it is in writing and signed by the party granting the waiver, and no such waiver will constitute a waiver of satisfaction of any other condition or failure to comply with any other obligation.

13. Counterparts: If the parties sign this agreement in several counterparts, each will be deemed an original, but all counterparts together will constitute one instrument.

14. Compliance with laws: Contractor shall comply with all applicable laws.

15. Entire agreement: This agreement constitutes the entire understanding between the parties with respect to the subject matter of this agreement and supersedes all other agreements, whether written or oral, between the parties.

The parties are signing this agreement on the date stated in the introductory clause.

University   **Contractor**

Signature: _____   Signature: _____

Name: _____   Name: _____

Title: _____

Exhibit 1

Index

Adams, Kenneth A., 2, 5
Assignment, 49–50
Attorneys' fees, 50–51
Automatic renewal, 52–53

Background/recitals, 16

Catering, 93–94
Collection costs, 53–55
Confidentiality agreements, 87–88
Contract-management software, 5,
    10–13
Contract review checklist,
    117–129
Contracts, generally
  acceptance, 3
  consideration, 3
  definition of, 2
  elements of, 3–4
  general purpose, 2
  legality, 3
  offer, 3
  technology, 5
Contracts, organization
  attachments, 102–103
  body, 102
  introductory clause, 100–101
  lead-in, 101–102
  recitals, 101

signature blocks, 102
  title, 100
Cost disclosure form, 25–26
Counterparts, 56
Court costs, 55–56
Credit and direct bill applications,
    88–89

Data entry and software, 108–109
Dispute resolutions, 56–57
DocuSign, 5

Entire agreement/merger clause,
    57–58
Exception memos, 109–110
Exclusivity, 58–60

Financial considerations, 23–29
Force majeure, 60–62

Governing law, 62–63

Hotels, 89–93

Indemnification, 63–65
Insurance, 65–67
Integrated library system (ILS), 13–15
Intellectual property, 85–87
Introductory clause, 15–16

Library license clauses
  access and authentication, 43–44
  accessibility, 44
  archiving and presentation, 44–45
  consortia purchases, 45
  copyright, 45
  course packs/electronic reserves/
    virtual learning environment,
    45–46
  geographical restrictions, 46
  informing authorized users of
    limitations, 46
  interlibrary loan, 46–47
  monitoring and reporting misuse,
    47
  patron record maintenance, 47
  return of/destruction of materials,
    47–48
  supplying patron records, 48
  usage statistics, 48–49
  walk-in users, 49
Limitation of action, 67–68
Liquidated damages, 68

Maintenance agreements, 93
*A Manual of Style for Contract
  Drafting, Fourth Edition*, 2, 5, 16,
  101, 102, 103
Model standard payable contract,
  129–134
Modification and waiver, 69
Multiple languages, 70

Negotiating, 103–107
Nonsolicitation, 70–72
Notice, 72–73

Online terms, 73–77

Payment terms, 39
Performers, speakers, lecturers, 94–96
Pricing models, 29–39
  cost plus, 34–36
  discount pricing, 32–34
  firm pricing, 31–32
Primary vendor, 77–78
Pro forma invoice, 26–27

Rebates, 36–39
Recitals/background, 16
Requirements clause, 78–79

Sample master lease for students,
  151–159
Sample preferred hotel agreement,
  141–149
Sample professional service contract,
  163–168
Sample standard amendment, 161
Sample visitor hotel rate agreement,
  135–140
Severability, 79
Shipping terms, 21–23
Sovereign immunity, 9–10
Supplier conduct, 79–81

Term, 17–19
Termination, 17–19
Termination/cancellation, 81
Terminations, 110–112
Third-party beneficiary, 81

Venue/jurisdiction/forum selection, 81

About the Author

COREY HALAYCHIK currently serves as head of content management at the University of Texas at Austin Libraries. He is the co-winner of the 2018 ACRL ULS Outstanding Professional Development Award and the 2017 ProQuest Coutts Award for Innovation. His work and research focus on improving efficiency, teamwork, and leadership skill development. He is also the co-founder and co-director of The Library Collective, whose goal is to redefine the professional development landscape for next-generation librarians.

BLAKE REAGAN earned a BA and JD from the University of Tennessee at Knoxville. He has an active Tennessee law license and has worked in higher education procurement since 2008. He is currently the director of procurement services for the University of Tennessee System. He is the 2015 recipient of the Young Procurement Professional Award from the National Association of Education Procurement. Blake also holds a Green Belt Certification in Lean Six Sigma.